The Missouri Botanical Garden's
SHAW NATURE RESERVE
85 Years of Natural Wonders

by Cindy Gilberg and Barbara Perry Lawton

foreword by Dr. Peter Wyse Jackson
preface by Dr. Peter H. Raven

MISSOURI BOTANICAL GARDEN
St. Louis, Missouri

Cover
Wild sweet William (Phlox divaricata) *flower in the Shaw Nature Reserve oak-hickory*
woodland, one of the best examples of native Missouri forest in the state. (Photo by Scott Avetta.)

Back cover
For eighty-five years, the Shaw Nature Reserve has sought to inspire stewardship of our environment
through education, restoration and protection of natural habitats, and public enjoyment of the natural world.
(Photos by Scott Woodbury, Catrina Adams, Danny Brown, and the Missouri Botanical Garden Archives.)

Page one
View from the prairie observation deck looking north.

Previous page
Sunrise on Pinetum Lake.

Opposite
During the biannual Prairie Day festival, cosponsored by the Missouri Department of Conservation,
visitors can tour a teepee and learn about Native American ways of life on the prairie.

The Missouri Botanical Garden gratefully acknowledges the following donors who supported the production of this book: Mr. and Mrs. Daniel A. Burkhardt, Mr. and Mrs. C. A. Case, Jr., Mr. and Mrs. L. B. Eckelkamp, Jr., Miss Mary Jane Fredrickson, Clifford Willard Gaylord Foundation, Mr. Robert E. Hansen, Kling Family Foundation, Dr. and Mrs. William S. Knowles, Mr. and Mrs. Charles E. Kopman, June M. and Fred S. Kummer, Jr., Mr. and Mrs. W. Stephen Maritz, Mr. and Mrs. John C. McPheeters, Mr. David T. Orthwein, Mr. and Mrs. Joseph F. Shaughnessy, Mr. and Mrs. Robert P. Tschudy, and Blanton and Peg Whitmire. Some donors wish to remain anonymous.

Photographers are credited on each page. Illustration on page 14 appears courtesy of the State Historical Society of Missouri; on pages 17 and 21, courtesy of the Missouri Historical Society; on page 19, courtesy of the Missouri Osage Historical Society. Other historical photos appear courtesy of the Missouri Botanical Garden Archives. Visit www.mobot.org and click on "About" and "Mission and History" to view an illustrated history of the Garden online.

About the authors
Cindy Gilberg
Cindy Gilberg (B.S. in Horticulture) is a landscape designer, consultant, teacher, and contract employee of the Shaw Nature Reserve. She writes a monthly column on native plants for the *Gateway Gardener* magazine. Cindy served as Midwest director of the Perennial Plant Association and is currently president of the St. Louis Horticulture Co-op. She was co-founder of Gilberg Perennial Farms in St. Louis, the area's premier retailer of perennials, herbs, and native plants for over thirty years.

Barbara Perry Lawton
Award-winning writer, author, speaker, and photographer, Barbara Perry Lawton has written extensively on gardening and horticulture. She is the author of over 1,500 articles and a dozen books for various publishers, including Timber Press, Fulcrum Publishing, Meredith Corporation, Ortho, and the Missouri Department of Conservation. She has earned numerous regional and national honors for her achievements.

Editor: Elizabeth McNulty
Designer: Andrea Androuais
Production assistant: Melissa Layton

Printed on 100% post-consumer recyled paper.

Shaw Nature Reserve: 85 Years of Natural Wonders (ISBN: 978-0-615-41544-4) is available at the Missouri Botanical Garden's Garden Gate Shop in St. Louis and the Shaw Nature Reserve's Visitor Center in Gray Summit, Missouri. To order additional copies, visit our online store: www.gardengateshop.org, or call toll-free 1-800-315-6307.

TABLE OF CONTENTS

FOREWORD

As we celebrate the eighty-fifth anniversary of the Shaw Nature Reserve this year, the mission of the Reserve—to "inspire stewardship of our environment through education, restoration and protection of natural habitats, and public enjoyment of the natural world"—has never been more critical. The year 2010 is the International Year of Biodiversity, designated by the United Nations to draw attention to the continuing devastating loss worldwide of tens of thousands of species—plants and animals. We need to celebrate biodiversity, but equally, we need to be aware that now is a time for action to halt its loss. Biodiversity conservation needs to become a common public concern, and there is no way better to achieve this than through experiencing nature in all its diversity in a beautiful natural setting.

Imagine the wonderful nature experiences possible at the Shaw Nature Reserve:

- a sixth grader's first night-time hike through the woods, hearing a deer snorting gently nearby in the darkness;
- a guided opportunity to learn the diversity of native wildflowers and trees that are so bewildering without an expert on hand to explain and identify;
- a group of high-schoolers using the latest GPS technology to conduct fieldwork at a college level;
- a stroll with grandmother in her wheelchair down the accessible paths and boardwalk in the wetlands to watch for migrating birds;
- schoolchildren staying in the Dana Brown Overnight Center taking a pre-dawn hike to watch the sunrise over the Meramec River.

These are the experiences that inspire new concern and action. They help us to make new connections with the natural world and inspire us to preserve the natural environment in which they occurred. They might encourage a young adult to join the next generation of scientists and conservationists—or

help us all to put the principles of conservation and sustainability into practice in our lives. According to writers such as Richard Louv, author of *Last Child in the Woods*, these experiences have become all too rare in our modern lives. The Shaw Nature Reserve is a great place so close to St. Louis where people can start to bring these experiences back into their lives.

The Shaw Nature Reserve is also an outdoor conservation laboratory. Prairie restoration projects begun thirty years ago are providing data on how we can better manage or recreate natural ecosystems lost in our relentless march toward so-called "development." The Reserve is a great place to study climate change too and provides data for collaborative projects with Washington University in St. Louis. Through my research I have come to the conclusion that if these predictions are correct, we could lose many of the plants and animals that live around us this century. We don't yet know what the causes of loss will be, and more research is needed quickly if we hope to combat the effects of climate change.

The Shaw Nature Reserve is also a wonderful place to study the connections between plants and people. What plants did the first settlers in the St. Louis region encounter when they arrived? How did Native Americans before them use these plants for food, medicines, and many other essential purposes in their lives? Going forward, how can we use and appreciate plants as our greatest renewable natural resources?

Eighty-five years ago, the Shaw Nature Reserve was imagined as a life raft for plants failing in the polluted St. Louis environment. Today, we are witnessing an environmental disaster on a global scale. Experiences at the Reserve will help us to find ways to remake a troubled world—finding new solutions and models to go forward together. Please visit www.mobot.org to join the Missouri Botanical Garden and the Shaw Nature Reserve in facing these challenges.

Dr. Peter Wyse Jackson
President, Missouri Botanical Garden

Left
The rustic gazebo in the Whitmire Wildflower Garden offers a tranquil resting spot from which to observe a diversity of native wildflowers, shrubs, and trees, including golden ragwort (Packera aurea), *ostrich fern* (Matteuccia struthiopteris), *and overhanging pagoda dogwood* (Cornus alternifolia).

PREFACE

The Missouri Botanical Garden had its origin in the dream of a visionary man, Henry Shaw, who wanted to create a legacy "for all time for the public good" in his adopted hometown of St. Louis. Opening to the public in 1859, the Garden was then well beyond the outskirts of St. Louis in a farmed area that had been tall-grass prairie "undulating in the gentle breeze," as Shaw recalled.

Only sixty-six years later, in 1925, the Shaw Nature Reserve (or Gray Summit Extension, as it was then called) had its origin in an environmental catastrophe. By the 1920s, St. Louis sat under a heavy cloud of soft coal smoke. Many plants at the Garden were dying from the fumes and dense soot. The Board of Trustees took action, purchasing several farms near Gray Summit, thirty-five miles west of St. Louis, with the intent of relocating the orchid collection immediately—and the entire Garden if necessary. Construction at Gray Summit proceeded apace; the orchid collection was moved; and an intensive planting of pines was begun, as most conifers in the city had already succumbed.

On Tuesday, November 28, 1939, the St. Louis skies were so dark with coal the streetlights had to be kept on all day. Black Tuesday resulted in intense public outcry. In April 1940, city government passed a stringent anti-smoke ordinance, and soft Illinois coal was banned from use. Home fires now burned Arkansas anthracite, which was a harder but more costly coal that burned cleaner. Within two years, there was no more discussion about relocating the Garden's collection. Plant life—and human health—had largely bounced back.

Plants, along with algae and a few kinds of bacteria, are the basis of all life. Through the process of photosynthesis, a small percentage of the abundant flow of energy from the sun is converted into chemical bonds. This stored energy makes the growth of plants and all other organisms possible, directly or indirectly.

Today, plants have become the proverbial canary in the coal mine. We are destroying their habitats; spreading invasive plants, animals, and diseases; and altering the climates to which the particular kinds of plants are adjusted. By the end of this century, half of the estimated 400,000 species of plants could be extinct in nature. The work of botanists has never been more urgent: to discover, document, and preserve the world's vanishing flora so the world of the future might be as sustainable, healthy, and beautiful as the one into which we were born.

The early-twentieth-century St. Louis environmental catastrophe had a positive outcome, but not before it first reached a nadir. We cannot rebound completely from the present catastrophic situation, but we can ameliorate its consequences by our actions. Botanical gardens are leaders in discovering, describing, and saving plants for the future, and the Missouri Botanical Garden is among the top gardens in taking effective action locally and in many different parts of the world.

Over the years, the Shaw Nature Reserve has found a new and vital purpose "to inspire responsible stewardship of our environment through education, restoration and protection of natural habitats, and public enjoyment of the natural world." Your membership in the Missouri Botanical Garden supports the Shaw Nature Reserve as well as the Garden's worldwide programs in conservation and education. Please join us in this great effort. Visit www.mobot.org and pledge your support.

Peter H. Raven

Dr. Peter H. Raven
President Emeritus, Missouri Botanical Garden

Left
On a day in late winter, flowers of Crocus tommasinianus *unfurl on the Bascom House lawn. The Shaw Nature Reserve is beautiful in all four seasons.*

INTRODUCTION

The Shaw Nature Reserve, on the Meramec River and about six miles south of the Missouri River, is in the area known as the Ozark Border. This region encompasses some thirteen percent of the state of Missouri and divides the rolling prairie lands of northern Missouri, formed by glaciers, from the Ozark Plateau, formed by uplift and erosion. The Reserve is near the junction of Highway 100 and Interstate 44 in northeastern Franklin County.

Missouri is known for its rich and beautiful collection of natural habitats as well as for its complex and diverse geology. Since the Shaw Nature Reserve sits at the juncture of several of these major Midwestern habitats, the diversity of both plant and animal life is great. This natural diversity provides an exceptional outdoor classroom for scholars and students as well as casual observers.

At the Reserve, the restored prairies evoke images of buffalo and Native Americans as breezes ripple the sea of native grasses and forbs. Each spring, abundant woodlands burst forth with a multitude of native wildflowers while, later in the year, the same woodlands offer lush green shade, a refuge from the summer sun.

Wetlands, known for their splendid array of species, offer a close-up look at aquatic plant and animal life. Visitors to this special environment include great blue and green herons, dragonflies, and other fascinating creatures. The slopes, which are the watershed of the wetlands, are cloaked in flowery tall-grass prairie.

The many trails offer easy strolls and hikes that bring visitors in close contact with these habitats. One can explore for an hour or a day—the variety of trails offers many choices. Benches along the way provide resting spots for quiet meditation and observation of birds, butterflies, and other wildlife as well as the seasonal parade of both flowering and nonflowering plants.

St. Louis is one of very few metropolitan regions that can boast of a nearly 2,500-acre natural site such as the Shaw Nature Reserve so nearby. The world-famous Missouri Botanical Garden, the governing body of which founded the Reserve, remains in the urban center of St. Louis. The proximity of these two attractions allows easy access for children and adults alike not only to experience the natural beauty of the region, but also to learn sound environmental stewardship through numerous educational programs.

The Missouri Botanical Garden's land purchase in 1925 began the legacy of the Shaw Nature Reserve. Originally established as a safe refuge for the plant collections from the smoke pollution of the 1920s, the Shaw Nature Reserve has played an evolving role in the community through the years: a nature reserve, a place to walk and hike, and a good spot for relaxing and for studying nature. It has become a premier educational, research, and habitat restoration site.

Over the years, tens of thousands of schoolchildren and adults have learned more about nature and the environment with the guidance of Shaw Nature Reserve's educational and professional staff. Teachers come to improve their teaching of ecological principles as well as to gain a greater appreciation of the natural world. In recognition of its worth as an educational resource, the Reserve was designated a National Environmental Education Landmark by the U.S. Secretary of the Interior in 1972.

Left
One of over fourteen miles of hiking trails at the Shaw Nature Reserve,
a footpath through the open woodlands invites visitors to explore.

CHAPTER ONE

IN THE BEGINNING...

There was the land.

Located on the northeastern flank of the Ozark Plateau, the land that would become the Shaw Nature Reserve dates to 425 to 500 million years ago, the Ordovician Period of the Paleozoic Era. Prior to that, volcanic activity formed the Ozark Mountains, one of the world's oldest mountain ranges. These ancient hills once were many thousands of feet higher.

The area also is called the Ozark Plateau because of the way the contours were formed. Water and wind erosion cut deeply into the ancient plateau, forming the bluff-edged streams and rivers that now run far below the original land surface. At the same time, the high plateau itself was eroding to such an extent that Precambrian granite now lies exposed in Missouri's eastern Ozarks at Elephant Rocks State Park.

Geology

The bedrock is primarily dolomite (calcium-magnesium carbonate) and limestone (calcium carbonate), along with smaller percentages of sandstone, sandy dolomite, and chert (a flinty rock that is predominantly quartz). The latter became an important resource to the Native Americans as it could readily be chipped into a variety of useful points and blades.

The Shaw Nature Reserve lies in Missouri's karst region, a land that features caves, caverns, sinkholes, and springs. *Karst* is a term derived from a region in Yugoslavia where this topography was first studied. One of the world's premier karst regions, the "Swiss cheese" configuration of the Ozark dolomite and limestone is the result of mildly acidic water eating away through joints and crevices to create spectacular formations in the soluble bedrock. Rainwater and carbon dioxide from decaying vegetation combine to form

Cold-front storm clouds gathering over the rolling meadows at the Shaw Nature Reserve, March 1956. Violent storms are a hazard of the region, where warm, moist Gulf air from the south collides with the cold polar air of the plains.

this weak carbonic acid. Over millions of years, networks of caverns have eaten their way through the Ozarks. At the Shaw Nature Reserve, there are springs and sinkholes that evidence this process.

In more recent times, some 75,000 years ago, the Wisconsin Glacier descended from the North, scooping, smoothing, and shaping the land as it pushed on halfway through what is now Missouri. While its oppressive weight did not directly affect the Ozarks, some remnants of plant and animal life that fled southward before the cold reaches of the great ice sheets can still be found in the region. For instance, beech trees and river birches that are usually found in more northerly climes grow

425–500 million years ago

Underlying rock of Shaw Nature Reserve formed.

14,000–8000 BC

Nomadic Paleo-Indians settle the Meramec Valley.

in some of the Ozarks' cool hollows, and arctic lichens exist on some north-facing rocky cliffs.

Climate

The continental climate of the Shaw Nature Reserve's region is deeply affected by the warm, moist Gulf air that slides northward, clashing with cold polar air that thunders across the plains. Tornadoes occasionally punctuate monumental thunderstorms. Another result is the hint of spring in January as temperatures rise to balmy heights of sixty or even seventy degrees.

Rainfall in this region is often as capricious as the temperatures, with an average annual rainfall of about thirty-eight inches. One year may endure drought and another might face flooding. Plant life is, to a great degree, an expression of the annual rainfall. Average annual rainfall of about twelve inches results in a flora of desert plants. Where annual rainfall is twelve to thirty-six inches, the dominant plants tend to be grasses. Where rainfall is over thirty-six inches, the dominant plant life is likely to be trees. The existence of various floras is strongly affected by periodic fires.

Geologist-explorer Henry R. Schoolcraft, traveling through the Ozarks in 1818 and 1819, discovered a mosaic of plant communities. Dense deciduous woodlands dominated the valley floors while oak, hickory, and short-leafed pine covered the hillsides. The uplands were a mix of prairie, grassy glades, and open-floored oak woods.

Fire

Although the greater part of the Ozarks appeared untouched by human civilization, the exact makeup of the land was undoubtedly affected in many places by Native American burning practices. Tree scars and charcoal layers in lake sediments suggest that many fires were intentionally set. The Native Americans appeared to have used fire for many reasons, including improved hunting conditions, improved growth and yields, and clearing areas for travel.

The region that would become Missouri occupies a fascinating ecological transition zone for the distribution of plants and animals in continental North America. Subtropical species of plants and animals push north into southern Missouri and species of the Great Lakes region push down into northern Missouri, with Ozarkian outposts in fens and on north-facing bluffs. At the same time, Great Plains species range eastward into western Missouri while eastern forest species push into eastern Missouri.

Native Americans

As best we can tell, the first humans (so-called Paleo-Indians) did not arrive in the Meramec Valley until some 10,000–12,000 years ago. Traveling in small hunting bands following their prey—mastodons and wooly mammoths—they were part of the eastward drift of Siberians who crossed the Bering Strait, which was dry in those times. Evidence of their existence is found in the Clovis points discovered in the Meramec Basin in association with mastodon bones. Clovis points are large spearheads, well-crafted with sharp fluted edges. Using them, the Indians were able to repeatedly spear the giant animals.

Photo by David Ulmer

Periodic fire, often caused by lightning, is a necessary part of the prairie life cycle. Native Americans intentionally set fires to improve plant growth. Today, periodic controlled burns take place on portions of the restored prairie at the Shaw Nature Reserve.

8000–1000 BC ·········· 1000 BC to AD 900 ·········· AD 900–1300

Archaic Indians settle the Meramec Valley.

Woodland Indians thrive in Meramec Valley.

Mississippian Indians build mounds in the region.

French illustration of Shawnee campsite, circa 1820. The Shawnee inhabited the Ohio Valley and engaged in territory disputes with the Osage of the Mississippi River Valley just to the west.

Osage chief Black Dog by George Catlin, 1830. Catlin wrote, "The Osages may justly be said to be the tallest race of men in North America."

Campsites of Archaic Indians, who lived in the Meramec Valley and foothills of the Ozarks from about 8000 to 1000 BC, have been found, indicating that they lived part of every year in cave openings and under bluff overhangs. They developed the *atlatl*, predecessor to the bow, an effective throwing stick used to hurl spears at game much smaller than the mastodons and mammoths that were now extinct in this region. They also became less nomadic and began to forage for wild foods and also cultivate food plants, primarily squashes. They invented bone needles and were skilled at tanning and stitching leathers. Evidence has been discovered at some sites indicating that they wove coarse materials into baskets and mats. These hunter-gatherers believed in afterlife. Their burial ceremonies were elaborate and often included weapons and foods designed to help the dead person in the next life.

The Woodland Indians probably descended from Archaic Indians and gradually took their place. Living in small villages and campsites on cleared terraces and bluff overhangs, these people developed pottery and baskets for storing food. They used chert as well as bones and mussel shells to make a variety of

tools and implements. As they perfected both their crafts and their farming abilities, they became more efficient, gradually beginning to make extra goods for widespread trading with other groups. Ozark iron ore was used to make axes for themselves as well as for trade with other tribes and groups. The red pigment of iron ore, first discovered near the Maramec Spring [sic], was a valuable commodity that was used in trade by the first century AD. (This rich iron ore would prove the basis for a substantial iron mine and smelting center founded by settlers in the 1820s.) Woodland Indians prospered until about AD 400, but during the next few centuries they declined until they disappeared around AD 900, leaving few signs of their previous existence.

Next to inhabit the Meramec Valley were the Mississippian Indians, named for their close associations with the great river. These culturally advanced people had come up the Mississippi and its tributaries, farming the bottomlands and building a series of towns that served as bases for the colonization of much of what is now the central United States. The great Cahokia-St. Louis political and ceremonial center

1200–1808

Osage Indians begin migration and come to dominate the Missouri River Valley.

1819

Henry Shaw first visits the site of the future Missouri Botanical Garden in St. Louis.

was created with its signature mounds, which also served as burial sites. These people grew corn, beans, squash, and probably a variety of other food and ornamental plants. They relied on the rivers for fish and mussels, important sources of food. Mussel shells were valued for their use as both ornaments and tools. Pottery and other clay items became an industry, with a variety of products used for home and for trade.

The Mississippians thrived from about AD 900 to 1300 before declining as mysteriously as had the Woodland Indians before them. The collapse of their civilization coincides with the arrival of the Little Ice Age, which occurred in the North Atlantic from approximately 1500 to the mid-1800s. This cooling period was characterized by expanding mountain glaciers and generally cooler temperatures.

Over the next few hundred years, a number of Native American tribes migrated through the region that now includes the Shaw Nature Reserve. Evidence of their presence was discovered in relic tools, weapons, and trading goods that have been found here. By the early 1700s, the Osage culture had come to dominate. The Osage lived in villages of rectangular homes built of overlapping woven rush mats over posts and framework. They farmed, raising corn, beans, and squash, and also went on hunting and gathering expeditions, sharing the food with the entire village. Family was extremely important. A chief would rule each village, the title assured by heredity; the oldest son usually inherited the position.

European contact soon changed the ways of the Osage as trade goods and practices were introduced, but the hub of Osage culture remained in southwestern Missouri until early in the nineteenth century. In 1808, they ceded all rights to their land in Missouri to the United States and moved west to what would become Oklahoma and Kansas.

Photo from Missouri Botanical Garden Archives

Monksmound, also known as Cahokia Mound, located in St. Clair County, Illinois, 1906. The Mississippian Indians (A.D. 900–1300) built hundreds of ceremonial mounds throughout what is now the St. Louis area, giving the town the nickname "Mound City."

Photo by James Trager

Arrowheads found through the years on the grounds of the Shaw Nature Reserve are evidence of the centuries of Native Americans who predated European settlers in the Meramec River Valley. Visitors may see a selection of artifacts in the Visitor Center.

1879

Bascom House built in Gray Summit by Col. Thomas Crews.

1920s

St. Louis suffers from coal soot and smoke pollution.

CHAPTER TWO

HISTORIC TIMES

Prior to the arrival of Europeans, the history of the Shaw Nature Reserve is gleaned only through archeological evidence since the local Native Americans had no written language. From the late seventeenth century onward, European flags were symbolically raised and lowered as distant governments juggled claims on New World territories, territories about which those distant countries actually knew little or nothing. The lands of the New World served as pawns of political power long before their true values were known. That these lands already were occupied by indigenous people was of little significance to the Europeans of that time.

Hernando DeSoto and his men most likely were the first Europeans that inland Native Americans met as the Spanish crossed the Mississippi River in 1541 and explored what is today Arkansas, Oklahoma, and Texas. In 1673, the French explorers Louis Joliet and Jacques Marquette were the first to describe the Osage, the only tribe that appeared to be native to the Ozark region. (Other tribes they encountered were originally from east of the Mississippi, but had already been driven westward as European settlers advanced across the continent.)

In 1682, Robert Cavelier de LaSalle explored the Mississippi River Valley. Believing that the Missouri River was the main stream and assured by the Native Americans that it was the pathway to the Pacific Ocean, LaSalle claimed the entire valley for France (although residents of the valley weren't aware of it). He named it "Louisiana" in honor of Louis XIV, the Sun King. Fur traders and missionary priests became the early explorers who mapped the land and streams and established generally peaceful terms with the Native Americans as they did so.

In 1763, France gave monopoly rights to the fur trade in the territory on the Mississippi and between the Missouri and the St. Peters rivers to Maxent, Laclede and Company of New Orleans, France. That same year, Louis XV (a lesser monarch than XIV) ceded New Orleans and the land west of the Mississippi to Spain to pay his war debts.

Although the Spanish flag now legitimately flew over this land, the French language and influence were dominant for many years. In 1763, at the end of the French and Indian War, the Treaty of Paris gave Canada and the lands east of the Mississippi to England. Land that would become Missouri, including the future Shaw Nature Reserve, gained new importance as the hub of exploration and trade for parts westward.

This territory remained under Spanish rule until 1800 when another secret treaty restored Louisiana to France. Napoleon hoped to revive the French colonial empire, but gave up that dream when he needed funds to prepare for another war on England. The result was the 1803 treaty that ratified the purchase of the Louisiana Territory by the young and vigorous United States.

Founding of St. Louis

In the meantime, Maxent, Laclede and Company was thriving on its exclusive rights to trade in the Missouri River Valley and country west of the Mississippi River. In December 1763, Pierre Laclede chose a high ground at the upper limit of ice-free navigation as the ideal site for a new trading post, eighteen miles south of the confluence of the Mississippi and Missouri rivers. He predicted that the new settlement, named St. Louis for Louis IX the Crusader King of France, would become one of the finest cities of America.

The following spring, Laclede sent 13-year-old Auguste Chouteau to the site with a crew of workers to begin building the trading post. St. Louis soon became the center of regional fur trade. Although

---

1925

Garden purchases land that becomes
the Gray Summit Extension (now SNR).

1926

Lars Peter Jensen, Garden arboriculturist,
named manager of Gray Summit Extension.

View of St. Louis from the southeast by lithographer John Caspar Wild, 1840. St. Louis had grown dramatically since the turn of the nineteenth century to become the dominant city on the frontier and the "Gateway to the West."

the Spanish withdrew the exclusive fur trading rights that had been given to Laclede, his business continued to grow and within five years was earning a fortune for its principals.

The region was now open to competition, and new European settlers and merchants surged in. The European arrival had a devastating effect on the Native American populations, including the Osage. While trade increased the tribes' immediate wealth,

Europeans introduced not only new technologies and different food sources, but also smallpox and other diseases to which the native population had not earlier been exposed—to say nothing of the treaties which forcibly disenfranchised the many tribes. By the 1800s, Native American populations had nearly reached collapse. Languages, customs, and, indeed, tribes were becoming extinct.

St. Louis was a town of only 1,000 in 1800.

1925

Construction begins immediately on greenhouse range for the Garden's orchid collection.

1926

Landscape architect John Noyes completes Gray Summit Extension master plan.

Within forty-five years, the city would be a major transportation hub with 40,000 residents. St. Louis had become the dominant city on the western frontier. Henry Shaw arrived in the city in 1819. He was only nineteen but, with the backing of English relatives and contacts, he soon became a major supplier of cutlery to the pioneers heading west. He would amass a fortune from his hardware and real estate businesses, retire at age forty, and eventually establish the Missouri Botanical Garden.

The legacy of the Osage in the state of Missouri is largely their complex of trails. A major Osage hunting trail led from the villages south of the Missouri River southwest to hunting grounds on the Arkansas and other rivers. By 1821, this had become the approximate route of the Santa Fe Trail, the important 900-mile overland trade route connecting Missouri to the Southwest. This vital commercial link served until 1880 when the railroad connected St. Louis to Santa Fe.

Just west of the Trail House, a wintery view of what is now known as the Rus Goddard River Trail. One of several Native American footpaths that cross the Shaw Nature Reserve, it was later used by early settlers.

In 1835, the first state road established in Missouri followed the older Osage Road to Manchester and later to Jefferson City. It subsequently became U.S. Route 50. When iron was discovered in the Meramec Valley, traffic increased greatly on the road between St. Louis and St. James. In 1837, the state of Missouri authorized a state road between St. Louis and Springfield that would become known as the Springfield Road.

Route 66, of musical and commercial fame, was patched together from Native American trails, the Osage Road (also known as the Kickapoo Trace), market roads, and woodland trails. It would become a major transcontinental artery. Today the old trails have become Interstate 44 (since 1985), previously Route 66 (1926 to 1985), as well as the general route of major railroads leading from St. Louis through and beyond Springfield, Missouri. In other words, that old Osage trail led right past the Shaw Nature Reserve.

Settlers Arrive

Missouri became a territory of the United States in 1812 and was named a state in 1821, just nine years later. Only two years before, the United States government began surveying the land, establishing counties and townships. This meant that plots of land along the Missouri and Meramec rivers now could be sold to the pioneering settlers. Between 1820 and 1840, all of the land that is now the Shaw Nature Reserve was sold to private owners with two exceptions. An eastern plot was reserved for a school until the mid-1840s, and a section in a deep ravine remained unsold until 1851.

Gray Summit was established in 1845 when Daniel Gray built a hotel and settled in the area where two of Missouri's oldest roads crossed. The Wagon Road, as the Osage trail was then known, and the State Road, which led from St. Louis to Jefferson City, intersected here, and the Missouri Pacific Railroad later joined the junction. The village was named for Gray and also for the fact that it was one of the two highest points on the railroad route between St. Louis and Kansas City. A railroad tunnel, now owned by Union Pacific, lies underneath the community to this day.

In the early nineteenth century, settlers had been

1932

Gray Summit Extension renamed
Missouri Botanical Garden Arboretum.

1934

Dr. Edgar Anderson, geneticist at the Garden,
establishes native plant collections at Arboretum.

1934-1935

Civilian Conservation Corps lays
groundwork for Arboretum's roads.

18 shawnature.org

Photo from Missouri Botanical Garden Archives

primarily English. During the 1830s, a wave of German immigrants began coming into the area. To this day, although many Anglo families remain, a strong German influence still exists in the region. The industrious Germans transformed the upland prairies and wooded rocky hills into farms, putting most of the land into cultivation.

According to government surveys found in Franklin County records, the Reserve land was predominantly oak-hickory woodland (a more open type of timberland, based on distances among trees and general descriptions by surveyors), with white and black oaks being the predominant trees (fifty and thirty percent, respectively). Some ash, elm, maple, and black walnut were recorded, along with basswood, river birch, and sycamore near the Meramec River.

Some two-thirds of Franklin County was still covered with timber in 1888, although records show that there were also native prairies and glades in the region. The settlers used the timber freely, building their cabins solely of wood from chimney to foundation. They sold whatever timber they didn't need and raised cattle, hogs, tobacco, wheat, and corn on the cleared land.

From the first white settlement until 1925, the Reserve land was used almost exclusively for agriculture. Deforestation, crop cultivation, and grazing caused many changes to the land and its vegetation. Erosion occurred in crop acreage. Grazing encouraged the shade-intolerant eastern red cedar at the same time that it discouraged many other native plants. The condition of the land soon reflected its use by humans.

State of Missouri, 1833. After two years of intense surveying by the U.S. government, Missouri became a state in 1821. Almost all of the land that is now the Shaw Nature Reserve was sold to private owners by 1840.

1935

Part of new U.S. highway 66 is dedicated Henry Shaw Greenway.

1936

Arboretum entrance and Visitor Center completed.

THE EARLY YEARS

The Shaw Nature Reserve, known today as the region's premier resource for environmental values and education, had its origin in an environmental fiasco of the early 1900s. Plants, as well as people, were suffering from the lack of fresh air and sunshine due to the thick blanketing of soft-coal smoke in the region. In St. Louis, the smoke became so dense that streetlights were needed at noon. During one particularly bad period, experts estimated that each St. Louis resident inhaled fifteen tablespoons of soot over the five-day period. They were not alone: by the 1920s, the air of industrial cities all over the world was thick with soot and smoke from the bituminous coal that was burned for power and heat.

Soot particles and sulphuric acid injured plant life, and the very existence of the Missouri Botanical Garden was threatened. Severe damage to plant collections, both outdoors and in the greenhouses, was reported as early as 1917. Because of the risk especially to the Garden's valuable commercial orchid collection, the Missouri Botanical Garden Board of Trustees began thinking about acquiring rural property.

Acquisition and Development

In 1923, the Garden's Board decided to maintain the city garden with its scientific and educational features, but to procure a large tract of land west of the city, well beyond the pall of industry, to relocate and save the orchid and other plant collections from the effects of the air pollution. To meet the financial challenge, the Garden would have to sell fifty acres of the Henry Shaw Estate, city properties that lay outside the Missouri Botanical Garden boundaries. Once they had put together a viable financial plan, Garden director Dr. George T. Moore and the Trustees began their search.

Looking for possible locations within a reasonable

Photo from Missouri Botanical Garden Archives

A variety of leaves from the Missouri Botanical Garden collection showing damage from coal smoke pollution, 1930s. Garden director George Moore was instrumental in promoting a local smoke abatement ordinance, but not before making plans to move the collection west if necessary.

distance from St. Louis, they spent two years seeking a site with a variety of requirements. It had to be conducive to growing plants hardy in this region, but also already have a good representation of native plants on the site. Since many of the plants grown at the new location would have to be transported from the city Garden, a good road was essential. The site also would need an adequate water supply, a variety of soils and topography, the presence of building material such as rock, gravel, and sand, and, finally, a reasonable price. After over a year of investigating properties, the search committee focused on Gray Summit farm country.

Just thirty-eight miles from St. Louis, the proposed land consisted primarily of worn-out farmland, but included both broad, level expanses and hilly areas with a variety of exposures. Bounded by public roads in three directions and

1937

Louis Brenner, Jr., under guidance of Edgar Anderson, lays out wildflower trails.

1939

Civilian Conservation Corps completes Jensen's Point in Pacific, named after Arboretum manager.

St. Louis Saved from Smog

St. Louis Civil Courts Building downtown nearly obscured by coal smoke pollution, 1930s.

In the fall of 1939, the pollution problem in St. Louis came to a head with "black Tuesday," a day that found the skies so darkened with coal smoke that streetlights had to be kept on all day. Public outcry resulted in a mayoral commission and the passage of a smoke abatement ordinance. Meanwhile, Garden staff kept monthly records of the hours of sunshine at the Garden in St. Louis and at the Reserve in Gray Summit. These figures demonstrated the effect of the ordinance. In 1925–1930s, the Reserve recorded 200 hours more sunlight during winter months than the Garden. By 1942, after the abatement, the excess of sunshine hours at the Reserve over that at the Garden was only 22 hours.

with a significant frontage on the Meramec River, the land was distinctly separated from adjoining properties. The site, six miles south of the Missouri River, is roughly the dividing line between the once-glaciated rolling prairies of northern Missouri and the unglaciated Ozark Plateau of southern Missouri.

Much of Franklin County, including the Shaw Nature Reserve, has the long, steep ridges characteristic of the Ozarks. Remnants of a number of glades, also typical of the Ozarks, existed. The soils included clay loam, sandy loam, and black river bottom soil along the limestone bluffs that line the river. Over 50 species of native trees already grew there, and over 500 different kinds of plants had been recorded. In addition, a large historic home, considered one of the finest in the county, still stood on a knoll southwest of what would become the Pinetum. Clearly, this was a property with great promise.

Over the years, the land had been sold and resold, consolidated and partitioned but, in general, it remained in the hands of the prominent families who were related by marriage—the Roberts, Jeffries, Crews, Miles, and North families. The exact history of those original several farms that the Missouri Botanical Garden purchased from Joseph North and Gustave Goedeke is complicated and involved just about every prominent farmer, merchant, and miller in Franklin County.

The original 1,300-acre tract north of the Meramec River that the Garden purchased in 1925 included the five farms owned by James B. Miles, William H. Miles, Victor R. Miles, Joseph North, and Gustave Goedeke. Prior to that, during the 1830s, the United States government had sold portions of this land to Cuthbert S. Jeffries; John Reed, Jr.; Thomas Roberts and two of his sons, Edward J. and John A.

First named the Gray Summit Extension, the property was not originally open to the public. Work began at once on three projects of great priority—the orchid greenhouses, the Pinetum, and the tree nurseries. Lars Peter Jensen, arboriculturist at the Garden who had trained in Copenhagen, was placed in charge of the entire Extension where he served until his death in 1941. Affectionately known as Pete,

Acreage

1925	The Missouri Botanical Garden purchases 1,300 acres in Gray Summit, MO.
1926	The Garden purchases an additional 323 acres along the south side of the Meramec River.
1969	Bradshaw property (4 acres) purchased.
1971	Bair property (197 acres) and Covert property (116 acres) purchased; Morton property (253 acres) deeded.
1972	Smith property (28 acres) purchased.
1977	Butler property (223 acres) purchased and Freund Center dedicated.

Total today: 2,444

1940

Arboretum officially opens to the public for the first time.

1941

August Bielmann replaces Jensen as Arboretum manager.

1942

Trail House built at Arboretum.

The first item of business at the Shaw Nature Reserve was to move the Garden's commercially valuable orchid collection from St. Louis. By 1943, twelve greenhouses held some 20,000 plants, and the business to the florist trade amounted to nearly $70,000 per annum.

he and his crew made provisions to store rainwater in an underground cistern (125,000 gallons) that still exists today and a natural reservoir, Pinetum Lake (6 million gallons).

The orchid collection moved to a new greenhouse complex on the site in 1927, and within six months, the improvement in its condition was described as little short of phenomenal. The success was due to unpolluted air and greater exposure to the sun as well as to the exclusive use of rainwater on the plants. By 1943, there were twelve greenhouses enclosing some twenty thousand plants, mostly the Garden's famous orchid collection. The business of selling orchids to St. Louis florists proved lucrative in the 1940s, providing a peak annual income in 1946 of $69,871 (nearly $800,000 in 2010 purchasing power).

1943
Over 20,000 plants, mostly orchids, were housed in the greenhouses.

1946
Serpentine wall constructed, based on design by Thomas Jefferson.

1951
Louis Brenner, Jr., named assistant manager of Arboretum.

The Original Master Plan

The original Gray Summit Extension master plan was completed by John Noyes in 1926. Born in Boston in 1887, Noyes attended the University of Massachusetts and had come to St. Louis in 1913 as a botany instructor at the Missouri Botanical Garden's School for Gardening. In 1914, he was appointed resident landscape architect, the only one in the history of the institution. Noyes would go on to design many St. Louis commissions, from schools to subdivisions, including Westwood Country Club, Mary Institute, Wydown Terrace Subdivision, and Pasadena Park Subdivision, to name but a few. Even after opening his own practice in 1920, he continued on the staff of the Garden. While he worked essentially within the parameters of the existing plan at the city Garden, the responsibility for the Gray Summit Extension was his alone.

Noyes' plan for the Reserve took into account the original intent of the Garden's Trustees to move all outdoor plantings to Gray Summit eventually. Thus, he included several areas of formal gardens, formal pathways, fountains, orchards, and buildings for display. There were sections for exotic plants, main display grounds, the Pinetum, orchards, a North American plants section, and experimental and service areas. The original work on the greenhouses and the Pinetum was in accordance with the Noyes master plan.

Photo from Missouri Botanical Garden Archives

Mules were widely used on the Missouri Botanical Garden's new Gray Summit Extension in the 1920s for everything from plowing fields to hauling gravel from the Meramec River for road rocking.

Lars Peter Jensen
manager 1926–1941

Photo from Missouri Botanical Garden Archives

Lars Peter Jensen, late 1920s

Originally the arboriculturist at the Missouri Botanical Garden, he was put in charge of the Arboretum upon its acquisition in 1926 and served until his death in 1941. By 1929, Jensen had overseen the building of the orchid greenhouses, planted 15,000 daffodils in the Pinetum area, established the Rhododendron Dell (no longer extant), and made a good start on the apple, crabapple, Japanese cherry, and nut orchards. Many of the daffodils, planted so long ago, have survived. Visitors were welcome in the orchid houses on weekends and holidays, but the Gray Summit Extension, as it was then known, did not open to the public until 1940.

1952

The Conservation Commission designates the Arboretum a game preserve.

1957

Frank Steinberg replaces Bielmann as superintendent of the Arboretum.

Bascom House

The Bascom House, circa 1890s. This elegant brick home was considered one of the finest in the area when it was constructed in 1879.

On a knoll overlooking Pinetum Lake, prairie, and woodland stands an elegant home. The red brick structure was built by Thomas Crews, a Confederate colonel, in 1879 and was considered one of the finest homes in the area at that time. The structure features 12-foot ceilings, a graceful walnut stairway, and skillfully carved Italian marble fireplace mantles. The house was very modern for its time with a bathroom on each floor equipped with huge built-in zinc-lined wooden bathtubs.

The Crews farm consisted of 320 acres of the original 1,300 acres of farmland acquired by Missouri Botanical Garden in 1925. The historic house was renovated in 1993 with environmentally sound practices and dedicated in memory of former Board of Trustees President Joseph H. Bascom in 1995. Today, the Bascom House is home to administrative offices upstairs. On the ground floor, "People on the Land," a permanent exhibit funded by the Missouri Department of Conservation, chronicles the impact of humans on land use in this region. Seasonal displays by regional artists and photographers are also shown.

Pinetum, Orchards, and Plant Collections

The Pinetum is approximately sixty acres near the main entrance. The central three-acre lake was created by Lars Jensen using horse-drawn equipment to enlarge the enormous ditch that bisected the site. It served both as a water reservoir for the greenhouses and as the major landscape feature of the Pinetum.

The crew, between 1925 and 1927, planted pine, fir, spruce, cypress, and juniper from many regions of North America, Europe, and Asia around the lake. Some 450 species and 22 genera of conifers were tested in the Pinetum over the next twenty years. The Pinetum supplied a vast amount of information about the culture and suitability of conifers in the area.

Other economic displays were attempted as well. Manager Jensen and his team planted a seventeen-acre apple orchard of 600 trees in 1927. The orchard included four or five of the best commercial varieties and was designed to be a demonstration orchard for regional farmers.

Nut orchards were established in 1929, and some 300 chestnut trees were added south of Brush Creek in 1932. Walnut, hazelnut, and pecan trees were added in 1935. However, nut trees need many years to grow before mature harvests can be realized, and the project would prove a long-term challenge.

In addition to useful plants, staff planted flowering ornamental trees and shrubs in several successive plantings. They established the Rhododendron Dell with some 2,120 plants south of

1958

Orchid collection moves from Arboretum back to the Garden in the city.

1960s

Rise of ecological and environmental studies at the Arboretum.

24  shawnature.org

Between 1925 and 1927, crews planted over 450 species of pine, fir, spruce, cypress, and juniper from all over the world around Pinetum Lake to test for hardiness in the St. Louis region.

the greenhouses and in the woods west of the Quarry Road. None of these shrubs exist today since the lime soil would have needed constant acidification to maintain their health.

Northeast of where the Trail House now stands, an orchard of flowering crabapples and Japanese flowering cherry trees—1,000 of each—was planted. It was magnificent in spring bloom, but the drought of 1930s damaged the cherry trees beyond recovery and they were removed in 1939. The crabapples persisted, but many were lost during the unusually cold winter of 1973. By the early 1990s, only a few remained.

Hundreds of redbud and dogwood trees were planted during the early 1930s and provided a wonderful display along trails and the margins of fields. This collection included such horticultural varieties as the rose-flowered and double-bracted dogwoods.

The Thirties

The continent-wide drought that led to the Dust Bowl conditions further west seriously affected Missouri and proved a severe challenge to the Gray Summit property. Water, for both irrigation and fire protection, became a primary concern. By the end of 1931, the 150,000-gallon reservoir was exhausted and the well-water level was drawn down from 25 to 65 feet. In addition to the drought, the country was in the hard grip of the Great Depression.

It is a miracle that anything was accomplished at the Reserve at that time; nevertheless things were moving along. Road construction began in 1929 and continued through the years, using the seemingly endless supply of gravel from the Meramec River. Three new greenhouses were completed in 1931. At the head of the greenhouses was a special display area, for years the only area open to the public.

Also in 1931, work began on the rock wall along Highway 100 that still stands today. John Noyes made plans for the Gate House, which would include restrooms and a large reception area at the main entrance. Completed in 1936, this building remains today as the Visitor Center.

In 1933, Garden director George T. Moore announced that the Gray Summit Extension would now officially become the Missouri Botanical Garden Arboretum. Although the property originally had been chiefly "a collection of cornfields," in his words, it now would contribute nearly 1,300 trees and shrubs to the city Garden annually. The Arboretum grounds were not yet open to the public, but hundreds of St. Louisans would drive out to see the orchid displays on Sundays and holidays.

During 1937, the first leg of the now extensive trail system was begun. With guidance from Missouri Botanical Garden geneticist Dr. Edgar Anderson, the Arboretum's assistant manager Louis Brenner, Jr., laid out wildflower trails in the areas where Anderson had been studying and planting wildflower species. Brenner worked on building the trails alone, as he said, like a cloistered monk on monastic lands. "I never saw a soul all day long for a number of

---

1965

David Gates named director of Missouri Botanical Garden, takes interest in the Arboretum.

Late 1960s

Renamed the Missouri Botanical Garden Arboretum and Nature Reserve.

The Dust Bowl of the "Dirty Thirties" created water shortages throughout the region. This reservoir was built in that era on the highest point of the ridge northwest of the Trail House. It was removed by the Army Reserves in the early 1980s.

Gate House with visitors, late 1940s. Completed in 1936, this structure is now known as the Visitor Center and houses a bookstore, restrooms, and reception area.

years." Meanwhile, Anderson's wildflower plantings were thriving: by 1934, he had established forty new species. Three years later, the Arboretum contained four radically different types of wildflower areas—glade, cliffside, meadow, and woodland.

The period from 1925 through the 1930s marked the first stage of the development of what would become the Shaw Nature Reserve. Over the years, manager Jensen became known as more than a mere arboretum manager—he organized garden clubs, preached wildflower conservation, sponsored banks of flowers and shrubs along Highway 66, and became known as a great horticulturist. The very survival of the Reserve during this demanding and difficult period is a tribute to the dedication, hard work, and outreach of Jensen and his small crew, as well as the persistence and support of the founding institution, the Missouri Botanical Garden.

The Daffodils

The daffodils *(Narcissus)* that paint the open slopes of the Shaw Nature Reserve each spring have been a major attraction for many years. Visitors come from near and far to be dazzled by thousands upon thousands of daffodils that bloom in March and April.

Many of the daffodils that appear each spring, providing a spectacular display especially along the slopes of the Pinetum, were planted in the 1930s and 1940s. Between 1938 and 1942, many varieties of narcissus at both the city Garden and the Arboretum were planted, evaluated, and studied by Dr. Edgar Anderson, who was especially fond of narcissus and devoted much time and energy to improving the Garden's collections.

1968

Andrew L. Johnson named Arboretum's head of program development, a new position.

1971

David Goudy replaces Steinberg as superintendant of Arboretum.

1972

U.S. Department of the Interior names Arboretum a National Environmental Education Landmark.

In the 1930s and 1940s, thousands of daffodils were planted at the Gray Summit Extension as part of Garden geneticist Dr. Edgar Anderson's breeding and evaluation program.

A friend of Lars Jensen, John Howe of nearby Pacific, was an amateur daffodil breeder and noted horticulturist. He sent a bushel of daffodils to the Arboretum, and when Anderson saw them, he considered them masterpieces. Planted around the Pinetum Lake, they became an important part of the naturalized bulb plantings. Anderson also obtained prize narcissi from other daffodil breeders.

The goal was to have a continuous display of color lasting a full two months by using a mix of early- to late-blooming varieties. The early varieties tend to have bright yellow flowers with long trumpets, while the later ones include more white varieties with wide, flat blossoms. The collection includes many cultivars and varieties that continue to be highly valued by narcissus experts today.

Over the years, the daffodils continued to naturalize at the Reserve, as daffodils will do, without much in the way of care and maintenance. To improve the vigor of the plants and the quality of the display, in the 2000s the Missouri Botanical Garden's lead bulb specialist, senior horticulturist Jason Delaney, undertook a multiyear process of digging, dividing, and identifying. Along the way, he and his crew of volunteers rediscovered a "lost" cultivar ('Icicle'), as well as many other rare and prized varieties.

Edgar Anderson

Dr. Edgar Anderson, mid-1950s.

Edgar Anderson first joined the Missouri Botanical Garden staff in 1923 as a plant geneticist. A professor of botany at Washington University and briefly (from 1954 to 1957) the director of the Missouri Botanical Garden, Anderson was afterward named Curator of Useful Plants and returned to his passion for teaching and research until his retirement in 1967.

Anderson was among the first Garden researchers to make substantive contributions to the Shaw Nature Reserve. Interested in plant hybridization and development of varieties, Anderson spent summers at the Shaw Nature Reserve in the 1930s, growing crops of corn and hybrid corn for study. He also established forty varieties of wildflowers there and had countless daffodil varieties planted. Upon his retirement, Anderson taught the popular "Dynamics of the Landscape" class at the Reserve for many years.

1974

Tuesday morning wildflower walks begin at the Arboretum.

1976

Renamed Shaw Arboretum.

CHAPTER FOUR

DEVELOPMENT CONTINUES

A new era of development began with the appointment of arboriculturist August P. Bielmann to replace the late Lars Jensen in 1941 as manager of what was then called the Arboretum. Bielmann, who would lead until 1956, was known as a gruff man of purpose who hoped to make the property self-supporting. Bielmann understood the interrelatedness of nature as well as the role of modern technology, and he took both into account as he tackled some of the Arboretum's ongoing problems.

He developed strong programs of terracing and mulching to fight erosion, a constant enemy of Ozark farmers. He also emphasized the cultivation of grass for erosion control and sought methods to contain runoff. The Brush Creek terracing project from this era held water so it could gradually soak into the land and proved to be an excellent example of a watershed-control program. Today's rain gardens are descendants of this flood-control method.

Working toward self-sufficiency, Bielmann continued to develop the nut and fruit orchards, established a working sawmill to make use of the standing timber on the property, and began running cattle as an additional source of revenue, as well as to help maintain the fields. He also farmed a few hundred acres south of the Meramec River, building a ferry to shuttle men and equipment across the river.

As an agricultural steward of the property, Bielmann promoted good land-use practices and conservation techniques as examples to area farmers. Some of the property was used on a sharecrop basis. He continued to search for the best ways to use the land. A conscientious farmer at heart, Bielmann's single-minded ambitions for the Arboretum on occasion crossed purposes with the scientifically oriented Garden staff. Further, some of his practices proved more expensive than he had

Brush Creek bottom, about 1952. Manager August Bielmann established the Brush Creek project to control flooding and erosion. Seen here: the removal of seedling elms, so that oak and hickory can flourish.

hoped, and so he continued to look for additional sources of revenue.

Looking forward to more engagement with the public, Bielmann designed and oversaw the building of the Trail House in 1941–1942. The completion of the Trail House, together with the Brush Creek bridges and the loop road, would allow the public to access the Arboretum as never before. Prior to that time, visitors had to stick close to the main entrance and were seen only sporadically on weekends, when they could tour the orchid houses, and in spring when they could view the daffodils and picnic in the Pinetum. Although there are no records of an official opening of the loop road, there is no question that people began to visit in greater numbers.

1977

Adlyne Freund Center dedicated.

1979

George Wise replaces Goudy as superintendent of the Arboretum.

August P. Bielmann, circa 1946.

Trail House dedication, 1942. Designed and built by manager August Bielmann, the stone-and-beam Trail House allowed greater public access to the Shaw Nature Reserve.

A man of vision and action, Bielmann mechanized the Reserve, reducing the manpower needs. He aimed to have the property self-sustaining and to that end, invested in a herd of cattle and a sawmill to recycle storm-damaged trees. The Trail House, designed by Bielmann himself, was constructed during his time, as was the Boxwood Garden and the Serpentine Wall. In 1951, Bielmann and Louis Brenner published an article discussing the vital role of fire in shaping Missouri's vegetation. At the time, the paper was widely criticized, even condemned, though it is now considered a classic in the field of fire ecology. In addition to understanding nature and the role of technology, Bielman knew the value of public communication and worked hard to popularize the Reserve with the surrounding community.

The Trail House, located in the heart of the property near the wildflower trails, is a large shelter with a manager's office (now a classroom), restrooms, second floor herbarium (now a work space), and storage cellar. The Douglas fir logs came from Washington State, and a local mason built the stone portions. Over the years, it has proved to be a popular site for classes and meetings as well as a gathering place for environmental groups. It is also an ideal site for family picnics and a central place for hikers to rest before heading out on another trail. It was named in memory of Garden Trustee William E. Maritz in 2002.

A boxwood garden was established on land in the north-central part of the Arboretum. Featuring seven varieties of boxwood, this garden was dedicated and opened to the public in 1946. Bielmann then directed a 649-foot serpentine wall to be built to enclose two sides of the three-acre boxwood garden and provide wind shelter for the boxwoods. Unfortunately, the site had drainage problems and, as a result, the boxwoods were lost. The serpentine wall, copied from one designed by Thomas Jefferson for the University of Virginia, was restored in 1997 and still stands.

1980

Tall-grass prairie restoration project begins.

1982

John Behrer replaces Wise as superintendent of the Arboretum.

In a bid toward greater self-sufficiency, manager August Bielmann established a working sawmill at the Gray Summit Extension in the 1940s. He also ran cattle on the property.

The Wildflower Reservation, a 400-acre wooded hillside, was largely the creation of Dr. Edgar Anderson, August P. Bielmann, and Louis Brenner. The trail system in the river bluff area was primarily planned and built by Brenner, but Anderson was the driving force behind the plantings and overall plan. It was perhaps the first formalization of the Arboretum's focus on native plants, a focus that continues today in the Whitmire Wildflower Garden, the collaboration with the Missouri Department of Conservation's Grow Native! program, and the Reserve's Native Plant School.

Bielmann and Anderson also spearheaded a program of public education at the Arboretum, with classes, tours, and exhibits. An experienced beekeeper, Bielmann established a "sixteen-colony bee yard" at the Arboretum in 1942. Bielmann moved honeybee hives throughout the Arboretum in the belief that this would stimulate the growth and vigor of wildflower populations, but failed to realize the vital role of native pollinators, now under active study in the natural habitats at the facility.

Other wildlife also began to recover at the Arboretum. By 1953, Bielmann and his assistant manager, Louis Brenner, were maintaining accurate annual records of plants for the first time. In 1949 the Arboretum began a quail cover program in conjunction with the Missouri Conservation Commission to study the adaptability of potential quail food plants and their value in increasing wildlife. A similar study of the ever-increasing deer herd was conducted, which provided valuable information on game management. In the 1930s, there had been no deer or turkeys on the property. By 1952, the Conservation Commission designated the Arboretum a game preserve!

One of the Arboretum's most successful examples of public outreach during this time was a three-day pageant, "Saga of the Meramec." Designed to show off the Arboretum as a model and testing ground for sound conservation practices, it was held in September 1953 and attracted thousands of visitors. In addition to demonstrating machinery for use in farming and conservation work, there were a number of exhibits on such themes as soil testing and game management. A play, "The Spigot on the Hill," written by Mrs. Patterson Gephart and produced by the Community Players, told the story of pioneers settling in the Meramec Valley and proved to be very popular.

The 649-foot serpentine wall was built in 1946 using a design by Thomas Jefferson. It originally sheltered a boxwood garden, but today serves as an attractive architectural curiosity.

The Lean Years

In January 1957, Frank Steinberg replaced A. P. Bielmann as superintendent of the Arboretum. Back in St. Louis, the Missouri Botanical Garden was undergoing financial straits following the construction of the interstates and the move of the city's population center westward. A retrenchment began, along with a plan to lure back the public through the creation of a futuristic new greenhouse (the Climatron®). In the late 1950s, the air in St. Louis was clean enough again that the orchids were moved from the Arboretum back to the Missouri Botanical Garden where it was hoped the collection could inspire visitation.

In the meantime, the Arboretum faced steep budget cutbacks, and Steinberg, who had grown up in a farming community not far from Gray Summit, had little opportunity to accomplish much at the Arboretum for a number of years. The new administration eliminated all operations not considered appropriate for the facility. There were both philosophical and financial concerns behind these radical changes. The cattle and sawmill were sold, and farming on Arboretum property was almost completely eliminated.

With a staff of only one full-time assistant plus a part-time laborer, Steinberg did an admirable job of keeping the 1,600-acre Arboretum (at that time) in good condition. Mowing was the greatest responsibility. They also sprayed, cleared, and provided routine maintenance of roads and buildings. The property was open to the public every day, but apart from the annual picnics for the Friends of the Garden, little else happened.

Photo from Missouri Botanical Garden Archives

Tractor-drawn "pollination station," 1942. Manager Bielmann established a bee yard at the Shaw Nature Reserve and wrote about the importance of bees in a 1950 article in the Garden's Bulletin.

Frank Steinberg
superintendent 1957–1970

Photo from Missouri Botanical Garden Archives

Frank Steinberg, 1967.

Steinberg lovingly and faithfully cared for and preserved the Reserve during a period when very little money was available. With a two-person staff, he managed to keep the roads open and the grass mowed so that the property, which was then about 1,600 acres, could remain open every day.

1991

Dr. James Trager, restoration biologist, hired to oversee native plant community restoration. Restoration of the Reserve's glades begins.

1991

Native plant specialist Scott Woodbury hired as head of Arboretum Horticulture. Construction of the Whitmire Wildflower Garden begins.

CHAPTER FIVE

A NEW FOCUS

A new environmental awareness emerged in the 1960s in America. An emphasis on domination of natural resources shifted to a new focus on environmental balance and on concerns for quality of life. Environmental pollution, the harmful effects of pesticides, and habitat loss for wildlife became important issues.

The appointment of David M. Gates as director of the Missouri Botanical Garden in 1965 marked the beginning of a new era for the Arboretum. Gates, the son of Frank C. Gates, one of the country's first ecologists, viewed the botanical garden not as a cultural center but as "a place of beauty, an island of elegance, a storehouse of knowledge and learning of plants."

Noting the increasing number of people visiting the Arboretum not only for recreation but also for study and research, Gates wrote: "The Arboretum is again becoming a scene of renewed activity after several years of almost minimal attention." A new role was emerging for the Arboretum: that of regional center for environmental conservation and educational outreach, as well as recreation. In collaboration with other organizations and universities, there was a growing program in applied ecological research as well.

A new position was created at the Arboretum— the head of program development—and Andrew Johnson was appointed to it in 1968. Mark Paddock, assistant director to Dr. Gates, took a special interest in the Arboretum and worked together with Johnson toward achieving these new goals. Their shared dedication, persistence, and belief in the Arboretum as an ecological treasure paid off. Increasingly, scientific meetings were held at the Arboretum. Scientists, teachers, and students in botany and zoology from the Garden and local universities used the property more frequently. Dr. Edgar Anderson's popular course, "Dynamics of

Photo from Missouri Botanical Garden Archives

Former Garden director, and Shaw Nature Reserve advocate, Dr. Edgar Anderson teaching his popular "Dynamics of the Landscape" class in April 1967.

the Landscape" met at the Arboretum regularly each spring. He and Kenneth Peck, head of the Garden's educational programs, gave workshops on field biology for science teachers of St. Louis schools.

The Arboretum's farm south of the Meramec River became the site of an educational experiment in 1969 when Washington University allowed fourteen students to live and study on the farm and have their lectures provided by visiting professors from the university. This was just one of the new educational outreach programs centered at the Arboretum. Additional funding in early 1971 made it possible for the Arboretum to continue its development as an environmental education center. Acquisition of two important pieces of land, the gift of the Morton property and the purchase of the Bair farm, had also been accomplished at this time. These additions further protected the

1993

Whitmire Wildflower Garden officially opens to the public. First phase of wetland complex finished.

1996

Bascom House opens to the public after extensive restoration. John Behrer named director of Shaw Arboretum.

Arboretum from the continuing sprawl of suburban St. Louis. The property now held title to 1.5 miles of frontage on both sides of the Meramec River, which was being used for both study and enjoyment.

Frank Steinberg, who began work at the Arboretum as a young man in 1927, retired as superintendent in late 1970, and continued to work two days a week as a volunteer. David Goudy, who had joined the Garden staff in 1969, became superintendent of the Arboretum. He reported that the Arboretum's renovation and development program was making it one of the country's finest centers for environmental education.

Progress continued as public facilities were upgraded, including the Visitor Center as well as the classroom and meeting area in the Trail House. The trail system was improved and expanded. Program developer Johnson created the Wilderness Wagon, a narrated hour-long educational tour conducted by trained naturalists, a program that continues to this day. The National Park Service utilized the Arboretum for its Summer Adventure Program, giving field experience to nearly 1,500 children. The Missouri Botanical Garden's Pitzman Program, which taught field biology to children, moved to the Arboretum, busing 360 children to do so.

David Goudy
superintendent 1971–1979

David Goudy, 1981

Appointed in 1971, Goudy served as superintendent of the reserve until 1979. The Missouri Botanical Garden Arboretum and Nature Reserve, as it was renamed, became the center of many new activities, including narrated tours, children's programs, field ecology programs for teachers, and horticulture career programs. Goudy pioneered educational programs in St. Louis City and County schools.

Established in the 1970s during the Reserve's education renaissance, the Wilderness Wagon continues today to offer hour-long tours narrated by dedicated volunteers.

In 1971, Peter Raven became director of the Missouri Botanical Garden, replacing David Gates. He would further the environmental focus and educational emphasis at the Arboretum over the next several decades. That same summer, superintendant Goudy worked with the Parkway School District in St. Louis County to develop a pilot program to use the Arboretum as a field site for the regular science curriculum. The East Central Junior College offered a two-year career program in horticulture with the majority of course, greenhouse, and fieldwork being held at the Arboretum.

Not surprisingly, in 1972, U.S Secretary of the Interior Rogers C. B. Morton dedicated the Arboretum as a National Environmental Education Landmark, one of only sixteen nonfederal sites so named. At that time, the education staff of four plus the staff naturalist

2000
Renamed the Shaw Nature Reserve.

2002
Trail House restored and rededicated as the Maritz Trail House.

2002
Missouri Governor designates a stretch of I-44 the Henry Shaw Ozark Corridor.

Superintendant David Goudy leads project teachers through environmental awareness exercises, 1970s. In 1976, the U.S. Department of the Interior named the Reserve one of the country's sixty-seven Experimental Ecological Reserves for use in teaching and teacher-training.

National Environmental Education Landmark plaque awarded 1972.

offered a variety of programs for school groups that ranged from studies of native communities to the making of maple syrup. Adult courses offered in the spring and fall included a variety of topics from wildflower identification to basket making.

In 1976, the Trustees of the Missouri Botanical Garden changed the name from Missouri Botanical Garden Arboretum and Nature Reserve to "Shaw Arboretum."

At this time the Arboretum was also selected by the U.S. Department of the Interior, along with the Tyson Research Center of Washington University in St. Louis, to become one of the country's sixty-seven

Experimental Ecological Reserves. Chosen because it included excellent protected examples of Ozark border ecosystems, the Arboretum and the total network of field sites would provide scientists with study sites to gain knowledge of how these ecosystems function.

In 1977, the Arboretum grew by 223 acres when the family of Mrs. Adlyne Freund expedited the purchase of what was then called the Butler property through the generosity of Garden friends. The Missouri Department of Natural Resources assisted in the purchase by earmarking federal matching funds for a conservation easement on the property. Located along the eastern edge of the Arboretum, the land consisted of woodland, meadow, and a small portion of agricultural acreage, including about a half-mile of Meramec River—and Brush Creek—frontage as well. The rustic stone lodge on the property, built as a hunting lodge by St. Louis philanthropist David P. Wohl in 1932, became a handsome center for seminars, teacher workshops, and

2003

Reserve bottomland forest along the Meramec River designated a Missouri State Natural Area.

2003

Dana Brown Overnight Center dedicated at Shaw Nature Reserve.

2008

Nature Explore™ Classroom opens at Shaw Nature Reserve.

College students at "the Barn," north side of the Meramec River, 1960s. In the 1930s, the Barn housed botany students studying corn genetics under Dr. Edgar Anderson. Later, Washington University ecology students were part-time residents until it was demolished in the 1980s.

George U. Wise
superintendent
1979–1982

George Wise, 1979

George Wise was named superintendent of the Arboretum in 1979, when predecessor David Goudy was promoted to a senior position at the Missouri Botanical Garden. Wise had master's degrees in ornamental horticulture and entomology and was the former director of the Awbury Arboretum in Philadelphia. During his tenure, the Shaw Arboretum, working with the Department of Conservation and the Missouri Prairie Foundation, introduced the first 48-acre tract of prairie. Wise departed to accept the directorship of the Memphis Botanic Garden in late 1982.

organizational meetings. Renamed the Adlyne Freund Center, today it has become a valuable asset to the Reserve's education mission.

By 1979, the Arboretum drew the attention of many of the region's most noted amateur botanists and wildlife experts, including leaders like Art Christ and Edgar Denison. Loyal nature enthusiasts such as Nell Menke, Betty Nellums, and Peg Whitmire were among the many others dedicated to the appreciation of the Arboretum. Wildflower walks, which had been held informally for some time, were now regularly scheduled throughout the year. Today, restoration biologist Dr. James Trager, along with volunteers Susie and Dick Russell, continue the walks, introducing experts and neophytes alike to the wildflower treasures of the Reserve.

John Behrer, who began his relationship with the Arboretum as a volunteer in high school in 1969, became superintendent in 1982 and director in 1996. He would lead the Arboretum into yet another challenging chapter of growth and development.

2010

Edgar Anderson Center dedicated at Shaw Nature Reserve.

2010

85th anniversary of Shaw Nature Reserve.

SHAW NATURE RESERVE TODAY

The 1879 Bascom House is approached through the meandering paths of the five-acre Whitmire Wildflower Garden. Dedicated in 1993, the garden is today the largest native display in the region.

What began as the answer to an environmental disaster—the thick smog of the early 1900s—has evolved to become a premier public attraction devoted to the natural world. In 2000, the Arboretum was officially renamed the Shaw Nature Reserve to more accurately reflect its nature and function.

Since the advent of the Industrial Age, the landscape of Missouri has been so altered that few people have any idea of what the land once looked like. At the Shaw Nature Reserve, a dedicated group of staff and volunteers works to restore natural habitats to reflect what they looked like in times before the land was plowed, logged, and extensively farmed. The Shaw Nature Reserve has become a place to study, hike, paint, photograph, teach, conduct research, and more— a place worth protecting for future generations.

John Behrer
director 1982–present

Photo by Diane Wilson

John Behrer on a porch at the Dana Brown Overnight Center, 2006.

A native of the Glendale suburb of St. Louis, John Behrer began his career at the Shaw Nature Reserve as a volunteer in 1969 when he was still in high school. Nine years later in 1978, after studying wildlife biology at Colorado State University, he joined the Shaw Nature Reserve as full-time staff managing educational programs and maintenance. The salary was $7,000, but included housing on the property.

Behrer was named superintendent in 1982 and then director in 1996. He has overseen a period of tremendous growth and development at the Reserve, including: ongoing prairie and glade restorations; installation of a thirty-two-acre wetland complex (1991) and the Whitmire Wildflower Garden (1993); the restorations of Bascom House (1995), Maritz Trail House (2002), and Freund Center (2003); and the construction of the Dana Brown Overnight Center (2003) and the Edgar Anderson Center (2010).

"This is a much more diverse place than when I arrived over forty years ago, both biologically and with respect to infrastructure," Behrer said recently. "The Reserve's success is a product of a dedicated staff, passionate volunteers, and generous donors who believe in our mission—a combination that will serve the Reserve well into the future."

To inspire responsible stewardship of our environment through education, restoration and protection of natural habitats, and public enjoyment of the natural world.

—mission of the Shaw Nature Reserve

From his desk, John Behrer can see the century-old oaks on the Bascom House lawn and beyond to the Whitmire Wildflower Garden and Pinetum Lake. This view has been in a state of improvement and transformation since Behrer became the Reserve's fifth superintendent in 1982 and director in 1996. A Missouri native, John had always desired to work for the preservation of nature. Since joining the staff, he has provided continuity and guidance for developments from the 1980s well into the new millennium, while staying true to the mission of the Shaw Nature Reserve.

As Behrer frequently notes, you cannot take the human element out of the natural ecosystem. In order to maintain a high level of biological diversity, human interaction and management must continue. Fire management, control of invasive exotics, and selective forest management practices are all examples of the ongoing interactions that take place at the Shaw Nature Reserve.

In addition to the intensive work being done to restore, replicate, enhance, and manage the rich diversity of native plants and animals, the Reserve has added more educational programs, including informal wildflower walks. Begun in the 1970s and led by local botanizers and native plant enthusiasts, the Reserve's wildflower walks offer seasonal explorations through this unique natural area. And from an appreciation of wildflowers cultivated during these outings came the inspiration for the Whitmire Wildflower Garden.

By the late 1980s the increase in the number of visitors and use of Shaw Arboretum gave credibility to its many activities and projects.

Above
Donors and visionaries Blanton and Peg
Whitmire pose with Scott Woodbury, who was
named the Whitmire Family Curator of Native
Plant Horticulture in 2006.

Opposite
Today, the Whitmire Wildflower Garden
features over 800 species of Missouri
native plants and serves as a showcase for
professional landscapers and home gardeners.

Local businessman Blanton Whitmire was contemplating what to give his wife for her 70th birthday. She was a great fan of the Reserve's wildflower walks, and he wanted to give her a special gift, something that would be near and dear to her heart, and one that would keep on giving. On her birthday, Peg Whitmire received plans for the new five-acre Whitmire Wildflower Garden at the Shaw Nature Reserve. The Whitmire legacy proved to be a pivotal step in the development of the Nature Reserve.

The 1990 master plan was developed by Geoff Rausch and Missy Marshall of MTR Landscape Architects of Pittsburgh, Pennsylvania, who prepared the master plan for the original Garden in the city in the early 1970s and have updated it at frequent intervals subsequently. The plan clearly outlined the importance of preserving the natural and restored areas of the Reserve while improving amenities for visitors. Scientific investigations and educational opportunities were strengthened. All improvements were carefully planned to enhance, not alter, the property while setting the stage for it to become a major resource for ecological education and a premier center for habitat restoration and native plant study in the Midwest. These improvements are ongoing, even in the present era.

Horticulture

Horticultural responsibilities at the Reserve revolve around the Whitmire Wildflower Garden and are twofold—to develop and maintain the garden for visitors while augmenting its use for expanded native plant education and outreach. With sights set on promoting the use of native plants in the landscape, horticultural activities also include the Native Plant School, tours of the garden, outreach projects and events, seed collecting, and growing of plants for the wildflower garden.

Whitmire Wildflower Garden

The mission for this garden is to bridge the gap between horticulture and ecology by promoting the use of native plants in the landscape. This is even more significant today with the promotion of more ecologically sound landscaping practices. In 1991, horticulturist Scott Woodbury joined the Shaw Nature Reserve specifically to develop the five-acre garden. "This area is not a habitat restoration project, but a demonstration area for natural plant communities," noted Woodbury when this garden was in its infancy. It was and continues to be a showcase of native plants suitable for use in home landscapes. In 2006, Woodbury was named Whitmire Family Curator of Native Plant Horticulture.

Officially dedicated in June 1993, the Whitmire Wildflower Garden is today one of the largest and most extensive native plant display gardens in the Midwest with over 800 species of Missouri native plants.

A wilder section of the Whitmire Wildflower Garden is a riot of color in fall with purple New England aster (Symphyotrichum novae-angliae), *white downy aster* (Symphyotrichum pilosum), *and yellow tall goldenrod* (Solidago altissima).

Above
*Whitmire Family Curator of Native Plant
Horticulture Scott Woodbury joined the Shaw
Nature Reserve staff in 1991. Today, he continues
to oversee the Whitmire Wildflower Garden and
leads the Native Plant School, the collaboration
with Missouri Department of Conservation's Grow
Native! Program, and other outreach efforts.*

Right
*Full of ideas for home gardener and landscaper
alike, the Whitmire Wildflower Garden features
both popular and lesser-known local perennials like
feathery bluestar* (Amsonia ciliata), *red buckeye*
(Aesculus pavia), *and Virginia spiderwort*
(Tradescantia virginiana).

Opposite
*The latticed gazebo serves as a focal point for the
Whitmire Wildflower Garden and offers a quiet
place to rest on a bench and take in the colorful view.*

This demonstration garden allows visitors to see and study many regional plants and habitats in a relatively small area. Design elements include paths, benches, and other structures that provide a place for visitors to stroll, sit, and enjoy the seasonal displays of wildflowers and wildlife. Meandering pathways lead away from the Bascom House down a gently sloping hill. Each turn reveals a new community of Missouri plants: woodland, savanna, glade, prairie, and wetland. Plants for these habitats are grown from regionally collected seed or from nursery-grown plants of known origin.

One aspect of native plant landscaping is to demonstrate how diverse plantings increase biodiversity. Numerous species of butterflies and birds have been recorded in the Whitmire Wildflower Garden, as well as a multitude of insects. As the garden developed, local deer populations began to take notice and were causing noticeable damage to some of the plant collections. Since their natural predators had disappeared, deer numbers had long been on the increase. The humane solution to this problem was to build a deer exclusion fence to protect the collections from further damage.

Spring Wildflower Sale

The first spring wildflower sale was held in May 1993 and continues on Mother's Day weekend each May to this day. Its intent is to offer native plants and information to the gardening public. This event showcases many native plants grown from local seed, seed collected in the Whitmire Wildflower Garden and on the Reserve property, as well as from Missouri native plant nurseries. Networking and interacting with native plant enthusiasts foster a great interest in and exchange of information on gardening with native plants.

Right

The Spring Wildflower Sale has been held on Mother's Day weekend in May every year since 1993. The largest native plant sale in the region, it attracts some 1,500 shoppers annually.

Photo by Ken Gilberg

Photo by Scott Woodbury

Photo by Heather Osborn

Above

The Native Plant School has grown every year since its inception in 2005 and today includes professional landscapers, as well as home gardeners. Over 500 students attended in 2009.

Opposite

Close-up of great blue lobelia (Lobelia siphilitica) *growing in the Whitmire Wildflower Garden, where over 800 varieties of Missouri native plants are showcased.*

Native Plant School

The Native Plant School was launched in 2005. Using the Whitmire Wildflower Garden as an outdoor classroom, the school offers in-depth information on native plant landscaping. Classes include sections for homeowners as well as contractors, developers, and architects. Incorporating native plants in both residential and commercial landscapes can enhance aesthetics and ecology. Native plants facilitate storm-water management, reduce pesticide and fertilizer use, and minimize the need for both mowing and irrigation. Gardeners increase biodiversity and reconnect with the natural world by using native plants, while at the same time adopting more sustainable practices for the future.

Education

The focus on education at the Shaw Nature Reserve had already gained significant momentum in the 1960s with the advent of public attention to environmental concerns and ecological studies. When Dr. David Gates, a scientist with a background in ecology, became director of Missouri Botanical Garden in 1965, he endorsed the further development of environmental education and conservation activity at the Arboretum. In 1972, the Department of the Interior recognized the exceptional outdoor education opportunities at the Shaw Nature Reserve with a National Environmental Education Landmark (NEEL) designation.

In the 1970s, the Shaw Nature Reserve aligned with the Institute for Earth Education to pilot the program known as Earthkeepers. This program of environmental education created and promoted a deeper understanding of and responsible stewardship for the earth. Log cabins on the south side of the Meramec River served as home base for Earthkeepers' overnight sessions. After the construction of the Dana Brown Overnight Center in 2003, Earthkeepers was replaced with a number of innovative programs providing a variety of topics for all ages.

A Shaw Institute for Field Training (SIFT) team spends the afternoon exploring the Shaw Nature Reserve using maps, compasses, and GPS units, completing field observations along the way.

Photo by Catrina Adams

Environmental educator Lydia Toth joined the Shaw Nature Reserve staff in 1987. Today, as Senior Manager of Education, she oversees all educational programming including school programs and public opportunities for all ages. She continues to spearhead a variety of new education initiatives such as SIFT and the Nature Explore™ Classroom.

Classes for both children and adults continued to develop, coinciding with a number of habitat restoration projects that greatly enhanced the Reserve as an outdoor classroom and laboratory. The need for a staff member dedicated to developing and coordinating the growing Education Department at the Reserve was answered when Lydia Toth came on board in 1987. Her strong background in outdoor environmental education was a perfect fit. By the early 1990s, the training of dedicated "Teacher Naturalist" volunteers became increasingly important in assisting staff with programming for the thousands of schoolchildren coming through the gates.

With a focus on natural history and ecology, young children to this day are introduced to the Reserve through programs like "Earthwalks," in which they explore nature through activities using their five senses. Since 1993, the Habitat Helpers program for fifth graders has been meeting on weekends throughout the school year to learn about ecology through hiking, exploring, and investigation of natural processes. Older students might explore different ecosystems including the tall-grass prairie, wetlands, ponds, and forest, or learn about early settlers in the "Living off the Land" program. It's not unusual to see students navigating

throughout the Reserve using maps, compasses, and GPS units. Teacher training offers opportunities for teachers to learn how best to use the Reserve to support their science curriculum at school.

Rounding out the educational offerings is a variety of family classes and adult programs, from casual drop-in programs to comprehensive weekend-long courses. Nature enthusiasts join expert naturalists on seasonal walks to learn about birds, geology, wildflowers, and trees. Those wanting a more hands-on experience can experiment with natural dyes, make baskets or wreaths, and sample nature's bounty in a wild edibles class. Families participate in night hikes, pond studies, and overnight programs. The biannual Prairie Day event, co-sponsored by the Missouri Department of Conservation, is enjoyed by adults and children alike.

Dana Brown Overnight Center

It soon became clear that new facilities were warranted to address the growing number of students and visitors. As part of the 1990 master plan, all departments at the Reserve were to have new facilities to accommodate the growth of projects and programs without compromising the integrity of the property. The ultimate goal of all improvements was to further the Reserve's mission of educating visitors about the plants, animals, and ecosystems of the region.

A key component was to build a new, larger overnight facility on the north side of the Meramec River, replacing the old, run-down cabins that had been used for Earthkeepers. A generous donation from the Dana Brown Foundation made this new center a reality. Groundbreaking on the Dana Brown Overnight Center began in 1999 with an official opening in spring of 2003.

The location chosen is easier to access—on the north side of the Meramec River and within the main trail system so that a short walk brings students to the prairie, glade, woodlands, or wetlands. Just west of the Freund Center, the Dana Brown Overnight Center consists of a group of skillfully

Tucked into the woods, the Dana Brown Overnight Center features four charming and historic log-cabin lodges. A spacious Assembly Building and modern shower house complete this well-used facility.

restored log buildings that serve as lodges. All of these were found within 100 miles of the Reserve and date back to the 1800s. They were carefully dismantled and rebuilt on the new site. David Hicks, the Reserve's talented master carpenter and construction manager on the project, used traditional methods and materials to reconstruct the structures as authentically as possible. These restored cabins provide a link to the past in a way that blends with the rustic surroundings and also demonstrate how to recycle structures and materials on a grand scale.

Also included in the overall design was the Assembly Building, which provided a meeting place and dining hall. The Adlyne Freund Education Center, which had formerly served as a meeting place and dining area but was now too small, was renovated as part of the project to provide extra meeting space.

Visitors relax on the porch of the Assembly Building. Since its opening in 2003, thousands of children and adults have stayed at the Dana Brown Overnight Center, participating in a variety of educational programs.

Teacher Naturalist volunteer Carolyn Gildehaus helps children explore the pond life caught in a net at Wolf Run Lake during a "Wet and Wild" class.

Today, hundreds of groups check out of the demands of modern life and check into the Center. Real discovery shows of animal and plant life replace televisions and computers, insect and frog songs take the place of radios and iPods. The fresh grassy ground is felt beneath wandering feet rather than hard concrete walkways, and seasonal changes are embraced. The essence of the teachings is to discover, understand, and appreciate the simple beauty and wonder of nature.

Shaw Institute for Field Training

For older students, the Reserve offers programs such as the Shaw Institute for Field Training (SIFT), a partnership with Washington University's Tyson Research Center funded by the National Science Foundation. This program offers upper-level high-school students an introduction to environmental studies and research. The goal is to increase interest in environmental studies and also to convey to the community ongoing research and findings in this field.

Continued financial support from various organizations has made it possible for additional opportunities such as internships for college students. The interns gain valuable first-hand experience and, at the same time, are an asset to the Reserve's Education Department.

Nature Explore™ Classroom

After Richard Louv's book *Last Child in the Woods* was published in 2005, it prompted a paradigm shift in educational focus across the country. At the Reserve, the message of the book gave more weight and credibility to the increase in education offered to families and young people. Louv clearly illustrates the direct correlation between a child's basic health and well-being and the need for children to have access to the outdoors. This concept of using nature as both a healing place and a place for educational opportunities initiated a campaign for outdoor classrooms.

In an effort to have "no child left inside," in March 2008, the Reserve established a Nature Explore™ Classroom, in conjunction with the Arbor Day Foundation and Dimensions Educational Research Foundation. At the edge of a gently sloping hill between the Visitor's Center and Pinetum Lake, the area consists of pathways and natural materials to stimulate a child's natural curiosity and desire to interact with the environment. Composed of a series of outdoor "rooms," children can move about in unstructured play. Along with the Nature Explore™ Classroom at the Missouri Botanical Garden, this classroom was one of the first in the country and has served as a model for the development of others like it.

While Louv focused on children, it seems likely that his findings apply to adults as well. Many of our health issues stem from a lack of time spent outdoors—walking, sitting, observing, and understanding the natural cycles. Nature's regenerative potential goes a long way toward improving our emotional and physical fitness. At all levels of education, curiosity in the environment is encouraged and is the basis for learning.

Student groups conduct fieldwork as part of a collaborative program with the Tyson Research Center of Washington University in St. Louis. The goal is to interest high-school students in university-level environmental studies.

The Nature Explore™ Classroom at the Shaw Nature Reserve was one of the first such facilities in the nation. It is designed to engage young children in the joys of nature and outdoor play.

Top
Restoration biologist Dr. James Trager joined the Shaw Nature Reserve staff in 1991 initially to assist with the prairie and wetland restoration projects. Today, he works to coordinate and advance a variety of ecosystem maintenance and restoration projects throughout the Reserve.

Bottom
The Missouri state bird owes a debt to a program launched in 1998 by volunteer Claire Meyners and friends. The Eastern bluebird (Sialia sialis) *was once a scarce sight, due to the loss of nesting sites. Today, with over 80 nesting boxes with high-quality predator guards, these birds of happiness are seen throughout the Reserve.*

Opposite
One of the most visited areas of the Shaw Nature Reserve, Pinetum Lake reflects the stand of bald cypress (Taxodium distichum) *planted in the 1930s soon after the Reserve's founding. Over time, the mission of the Reserve has evolved to embrace restoration of natural habitats.*

Habitat Restoration and Management

The natural beauty encountered today at the Shaw Nature Reserve is the result of decades of active habitat restoration projects. Beginning in 1980, staff at the Reserve began work on the creation of a large prairie on former pastureland with the assistance of the Missouri Department of Conservation and the Missouri Prairie Foundation. Today, visitors to the Reserve can walk through over 250 acres of mature tall-grass prairie and perhaps catch a glimpse of what early European settlers might have found in the region.

The success of this project—and the successful partnerships it advanced—led to the expansion of other restoration projects, including glades and woodlands that exist within the boundaries of the property. Restoration and enhancement of habitats at the Reserve became one of the top priorities in the 1980s and 1990s. Director John Behrer initiated the construction of a wetland complex, which today flourishes with an abundance of life while providing a wealth of opportunities to observe and learn about wetlands.

Restoration biologist Dr. James Trager joined the Reserve staff in 1991 to concentrate on and orchestrate several of these projects. Formally trained as an entomologist, he is a naturalist at heart, eagerly doing fieldwork and teaching. The bulk of his attention is on habitat management, which is essential to maintain the diverse ecological associations that are present in the Reserve.

There is no instant gratification in this type of work as it may take five, ten, or even twenty years to achieve a mature community. Well-timed management is an ongoing task that includes prescribed burning, carefully timed mowing, sowing seed of under-represented native species, and control of invasive species.

Photo by Jack Jennings

Missouri Ecosystems

Today, the communities at the Shaw Nature Reserve form a mosaic of textures and colors, of plants and animals, that transforms with each season.

Glades

A short walk west from the Maritz Trail House leads through an open oak-hickory woodland to Crescent Knoll Glade. There, the Crescent Knoll Overlook provides sweeping views of one of the most fragile and unusual plant communities: a dolomite glade. Thin, rocky topsoil combined with outcroppings of shallow bedrock creates a challenging environment in which a diverse and colorful garden of wildflowers flourishes in the sunny space. Found primarily on south- and southwest-facing slopes in the Ozark highlands, an area where eastern deciduous woodlands meet the western grasslands, glades are categorized according to the exposed bedrock that exists in a particular site. Each has a specific population of plants and animals associated with it. In Missouri, the variety of bedrock includes sandstone, shale, limestone, dolomite, chert, granite, and rhyolite. The Shaw Nature Reserve's glades overlie Ordovician dolomite 450 million years old.

Glades are among the most unique—and fragile—ecosystems in Missouri. A variety of hardy wildflowers, but few trees, thrive in these sunny spaces with their thin, rocky topsoil punctuated by bedrock.

"We stood a moment to contemplate the sublime and beautiful scene before us, which was such an assembly of rocks and water—of hill and valley—of verdant woods and naked peaks—of native fertility and barren magnificence..."
– Henry Rowe Schoolcraft (describing the Ozarks in 1819)

The ongoing glade restoration has a goal of opening up overgrown glade areas to allow glade-specialized plants and animals to thrive. With the passage of time and the absence of fire, areas with thin soil that were originally open glades tend to close up, eastern red cedar *(Juniperus virginiana)* and redbud *(Cercis canadensis)* being among the first and most aggressive colonists. Staff and volunteers remove invasives and monitor continuously for other unwanted species. If this is done, native herbs often burst forth in unsuspected glory to the delight of naturalists and other visitors.

About fifty acres of rocky, almost treeless glades occur at the Shaw Nature Reserve. Thirty-five or more additional acres remain hidden by cedar forest that invaded the glades in the wake of overgrazing followed by decades of fire suppression. A cedar removal program launched in 1991 is restoring these unique spaces and allowing the species they host to flourish.

Above
A black swallowtail (Papilo polyxenes asterius) *alights on a western wallflower* (Erysimum capitatum). *The blooming waves of wildflowers attract dozens of butterfly species and other pollinating insects.*

Left
With their thin, rocky soil and lack of tree cover, glades tend to be hot and dry, and thus feature tough, drought-tolerant plants such as these glade coneflowers (Echinacea simulata).

Opposite
The Crescent Knoll Overlook provides sweeping vistas of the acres of glade flora and the Meramec River Valley. It is often sunny in any season.

The Shaw Nature Reserve is at the northeastern limit of one of Missouri's most extensive glade regions. Approximately seventy-five acres of these sun-loving glades exist on the Shaw Nature Reserve. Decades of fire suppression allowed cedar trees to encroach into the glades, thus starving the natural vegetation of light and preventing it from thriving. Restoration management began in 1991, starting with the removal of cedar trees followed by regular prescribed burns. Areas of cedar growth, obvious in aerial views of the property, indicate other glades that exist. These too are part of the active glade restoration projects. Populations of many glade species are flourishing once again.

South from the Trail House is a more intimate walk that winds through the glade habitat. A boardwalk, built from the cedars removed during restoration, ensures that foot traffic will not harm the delicate ecosystem. The changing seasons offer a parade of flowering plants, birds, insects, and other animals, many of which are specific to the glade habitat. Broad strokes of color highlight the scene with a

palette that includes red Indian paintbrush *(Castilleja coccinea)*, yellow Missouri evening primrose *(Oenothera macrocarpa)*, pink glade coneflowers *(Echinacea simulata)*, and orange western wallflower *(Erysimum capitatum)* in spring.

Lilac-colored spikes of blazing stars *(Liatris cylindracea)* punctuate the mid- to late-summer scene in contrast to orange clusters of butterfly weed flowers *(Asclepias tuberosa)* and the yellow discs of glade coneflower *(Rudbeckia missouriensis)*. In autumn, grasses bloom and bear seed before turning to tawny gold in late fall. Yellow prairie dock *(Silphium terebinthinaceum)*, goldenrod *(Solidago nemoralis)*, russet-colored little bluestem *(Schizachyrium scoparium)*, and pink glade onion *(Allium stellatum)* all add color late in the season plus much sought-after pollen and nectar for butterflies and other pollinating insects. One of the last to bloom, cerulean blue flowers of aromatic aster *(Symphyotrichum oblongifolium)* reflect the blue autumn sky. As winter sets in, many species of birds come to feast on the ripe and abundant seeds.

Prairie

Prairies expanded throughout central North America as the glaciers of the last Ice Age retreated. *Prairie*, from a French word for meadow, is a distinctive ecosystem that is mostly devoid of trees and dominated by grasses and forbs (herbaceous flowering perennials). The matrix of life in a prairie is a rich mix of plants and animals.

This vast grassland was home to many tribes of Native Americans who wove paths across the prairie, following bison, elk, and deer as well as the seasonal foods, fibers, and medicines that the plants provided. These early inhabitants observed benefits of fire in attracting large grazing animals and subsequently developed a "fire culture" to stimulate new growth on grasses and forbs.

In the Central United States, nearly unbroken, mostly deciduous forests extend from the Atlantic Coast to approximately the Indiana-Illinois border. Increasingly extensive patches of tall-grass prairie appear as one moves westward, giving way to a situation in most of Iowa, western Missouri, Kansas, Nebraska, and most of Oklahoma where tall-grass prairie was once the dominant vegetation over thousands of square miles. Prairies historically were maintained by a combination of climate, grazing, and periodic fire. Perennial prairie plants often have strong and deep root networks that enable them to survive drought and fire above ground. These roots also make them ideal for repetitive grazing.

Prairie blazing star (Liatris pycnostachya) *forms dense patches with magenta-pink flowering spikes in the Reserve's prairie restorations. Native field mice eat the plants' tubers, eventually thinning the blazing star colonies, but not before the plants shed myriad, windblown seeds that colonize and form dense populations in new sections of the prairie.*

Photo by Bill Davit

Photo by James Trager

Right

A brown-banded bumblebee (Bombus griseicollis) *about to light on butterfly milkweed* (Asclepias tuberosa), *the bee's proboscis already unfurling in anticipation of its nectar harvest. Approximately 150 species of native bees are among the variety of pollinators of the Reserve's numerous showy flowering plant species, part of the symbiotic diversity of plant and animal life at the Reserve.*

Opposite

Grasses and forbs are the heart of the prairie. When restoration was begun in 1980, only eight prairie species were commercially available. Today, there are hundreds, as well as the seed that is routinely swapped among institutions and restoration projects.

As Europeans began to migrate westward, they encountered this landscape, one unlike any in their homelands. They saw before them a seemingly endless ocean of grasses. Henry Shaw, who founded the Missouri Botanical Garden, wrote later of the first time he ever saw the property. In 1819, he rode out on horseback southwest of the city of St. Louis where he found tall grasses "undulated by the gentle breezes of spring." Settlers soon discovered that the rich loamy soil of the prairie would sustain not only cattle, but also major agricultural crops. This eventually led to the clearing of all of the original tall-grass prairie, with only small remnants surviving.

Most of the remaining prairies in Missouri occur in northern and western regions. A very few remain in the eastern section. No prairie remnants existed on the Shaw Nature Reserve property. Other than the taller vegetation at the edges of the glades, no prairie seems to have occurred within the area of the Reserve. Nonetheless, consistent with the Reserve's role as a

refuge for eastern Missouri's varied vegetation, staff began active prairie restoration on what had been fescue pasture and agricultural cropland. In 1980, in cooperation with the Missouri Prairie Foundation and Missouri Department of Conservation, approximately forty-eight acres of land was converted, the first prairie project on the property.

The original seed mix comprised four species of grasses and four forb species, the only ones available commercially at the time. As new prairie areas were planted, seed collecting from local sources became the main source for many other species. Today, over 200 species are represented in the Reserve's prairie plantings. All seed is carefully collected and cleaned by hand with the assistance of many dedicated volunteers.

Other prairie plantings have been established on the Reserve using in large part the seed collected from both the original prairie projects and from local remnant prairies. Taking advantage of the rolling hills, these plantings display plant species typical of lower,

Photo by Scott Avetta

Photo by Kyle Spradley

Photo by Danny Brown

Photo by Danny Brown

Above and left
Red-shouldered hawks (Buteo lineatus) *and red foxes* (Vulpes vulpes) *are just two of several predators that enjoy foraging in the prairie grasses where they hunt small mammals such as mice, voles, and rabbits.*

Opposite
Little sod house on the winter prairie. Starkly beautiful in all four seasons, the restored prairie at the Shaw Nature Reserve is preserved through careful management and prescribed burns. In the background, the authentic sod house of the type used by early European settlers was built in 2004.

wetter prairies as well as those of drier upland prairies.

Today, prairie plantings at the Reserve total approximately 250 acres and serve as demonstration areas to teach others about prairie ecology and about establishing prairie plantings. This large area of established prairie provides not only diversity of plants but of animals too. Insects abound, pollinating flowers, eating plants and each other. They in turn become welcome meals for amphibians, reptiles, and birds that forage for the protein insects offer. Mammals such as mice, voles, rabbits, and fox browse, graze, and hunt the prairie floor while overhead hawks call out as they circle with watchful eyes.

Whether seen on a late summer evening with long light dancing on the tops of flowering grasses and forbs or on a cool, foggy morning in fall, the panoramic view from the observation platform at the top of the main prairie is a grand sight. The sounds of the wind in the grasses and bird, frog, and insect songs serve as splendid accompaniments.

Thanks to the continued effort of conservation groups, prairies are once again becoming a familiar sight in the Midwest through management of remnant prairies and establishment of new prairies. In addition, the Shaw Nature Reserve has served as an exemplar in the use of prairie plantings in sustainable landscape practices such as highway plantings, commercial properties, and even on small residential lots.

Wetlands

Pre-settlement Missouri boasted approximately four to five million acres of wetlands. Since then, rivers have been channeled and wetlands drained and converted to agricultural and commercial use. Wet places, such as marshes, streams, and lakes, are especially rich in biodiversity. Among the most productive ecosystems in the world, wetlands provide critical habitat for a wide array of plants and wildlife. In addition, they serve as temporary storage of floodwater, aid in filtering pollutants, and help prevent soil erosion.

Since the 1990s, recognition of wetland benefits has resulted in the restoration and reestablishment of wetlands across the United States. Today, Missouri has thousands of acres of various types of wetlands, some of which are represented at the Shaw Nature Reserve. Deciduous forest dominates the banks and low areas along the Meramec River, and there are permanent ponds including Pinetum Lake, Mirror Lake, and Wolf Run Lake, as well as seasonally wet meadows.

Development of the Reserve's thirty-two-acre wetland complex and boardwalk began in 1991 on what was once a hayfield along the Brush Creek riparian corridor. The hayfield was reworked into a system of eight ponds and a low, wet meadow supporting a rich array of pond, marsh, and wet prairie species. The adjacent uplands that provide the watershed for the wetlands consist mainly of prairie plantings.

Development began in 1991, and today this thirty-two-acre complex at the Shaw Nature Reserve is a mature wetland, one of the most diverse ecosystems on the planet, and plays home to hundreds of species of plants, insects, birds, amphibians, fish, and mammals.

Photo by Sonya Buerck

Above and Opposite

A 300-foot boardwalk passes through swampy woods and marsh, home to numerous rare sedge and wetland grass species and to broadleaf beauties such as blue flag iris (Iris virginica *var.* shrevei), *queen-of-the-prairie* (Filipendula rubra), *and blue bottle gentian* (Gentiana andrewsii). *Water lilies* (Nymphaea tuberosa), *rose turtlehead* (chelone obliqua), *jewelweed* (Impatiens capensis), *and rose mallow* (Hibiscus lasiocarpus) *are overarched by swamp tupelo* (Nyssa Aquatica) *and bald cypress* (Taxodium distichum).

Funded through generous private donors, a grant from the U.S. Fish and Wildlife Service, and with the technical assistance from the Natural Resource Conservation Service, the Shaw Nature Reserve staff and volunteers established wetland plants in a constructed collection of ponds, sedge meadow, ephemeral pools, and wet prairie.

Seed was collected from wetland sites in eastern Missouri, including some species from Mingo Swamp Wildlife Refuge, in an effort to create plantings using regional ecotypes. The wet years of the early 1990s coincided with the completion of the first phase of construction, and the wetlands quickly filled. Soon thousands of amphibians, reptiles, insects, and numerous species of birds populated the ponds and moist meadows. The wetland complex now serves to educate and increase appreciation of the intricate nature of wetland habitats.

Sedges (*Carex* spp.), rushes (*Juncus* spp.), and bulrushes (*Scirpus* spp.) form the matrix of wetlands—they are to the wetland what grasses are to the prairie. Bald cypress *(Taxodium distichum)*, water tupelo *(Nyssa aquatica)*, and willow oak *(Quercus phellos)* are trees typical of

Above

The wetlands provide rich habitats for both plants and animals and form an important part of ecology education at the Reserve. Schoolchildren net tadpoles for pond class. Red-eared sliders (Trachemys scripta elegans) and greenfrogs (Rana clamitans) are just two of several wetland species of reptiles and amphibians. Insects include dragonflies, top predators among the diverse insects of wetlands, such as this widow skimmer (Libellula luctuosa).

Opposite

Brush Creek Trail Bridge provides an all-weather crossing to various habitats, including wetland loss mitigation ponds near Brush Creek that are rich in species. These are additional examples of the Reserve's commitment to giving visitors opportunities to see native Missouri flora and fauna up-close in wetland habitats.

wetlands, accenting the edges along with colonies of buttonbush *(Cephalanthus occidentalis)*, cordgrass *(Spartina pectinata)*, rose mallow *(Hibiscus lasiocarpus)*, swamp milkweed *(Asclepias incarnata)*, and copper iris and blue flag *(Iris fulva* and *I. virginica)*.

Plants associated with wetlands have evolved to tolerate both spring floods and summer droughts. It is, in fact, beneficial to many plant and animal species to have these alternating periods of inundation and drying out. For example, salamander and frog species are found in the spring ephemeral pools, coming there to breed and lay eggs, free from predation by fish.

The boardwalk provides an intimate view of the wetland's complex web of life. Red-wing blackbirds call from the grassy margins and, along the shoreline, herons patiently watch the water as they hunt for small fish and amphibians. Dragonflies and damselflies dart above water lilies and rest on tall stalks of rushes. Butterflies and hummingbirds forage for nectar here as well. As dusk falls, bats appear—aerial acrobats that dive and swoop as they eat their weight in mosquitoes each night. The Shaw Nature Reserve is on the Mississippi Flyway, and many migrating birds are recorded during spring and fall, including grebes, mergansers, bitterns, and several kinds of ducks.

Photo by Scott Avetta

Woodlands

Wildflower enthusiasts from near and far come each spring to visit the woodlands at the Shaw Nature Reserve. The subdued tones of winter give way to a colorful array of spring flowers—bluebells *(Mertensia virginica)*, mayapples *(Podophyllum peltatum)*, Jacob's ladder *(Polemonium reptans)*, and wakerobin *(Trillium* spp.) are just a few that bloom beneath understory trees like dogwood *(Cornus florida)*, redbud *(Cercis canandensis)*, and serviceberry *(Amelanchier arborea)*. In summer, students and hikers seek the welcome shade from the summer sun. Fall brings yet another spectacular show as yellow sunflowers *(Helianthus* spp.) and blue asters *(Symphyotrichum* spp.) carpet parts of the more open woods. Red, orange, and yellow foliage provide a final blaze of color before the woodlands once again return to a winter scene.

Where prairie meets these woodlands, there are fewer, more widely spaced trees. The more open canopy allows for the growth of grasses and other forbs not found in dense woodland. Having a park-like appearance, this boundary between the grasslands and denser forest has a high diversity of wildlife as well as plants.

Often fiery in the fall, oak-hickory woodlands dominate the Shaw Nature Reserve's vegetation. About ten oaks and five hickories make up the majority of species, complemented by a diversity of other trees, plants, fungi, and animals.

Photo by Brian Mueller

Above

The woodland is especially beautiful from March to June, with a succession of over 250 species of wildflowers blooming in varied habitats. In April, bluebells (Mertensia virginica) *blanket the river-bottom woodlands as far as the eye can see.*

Opposite

The glorious old oak-hickory forest at the Reserve shades softly rolling hills and meandering streams. In 2003, the state of Missouri designated 147 acres of bottomland forest and gravel bars along the Meramec River a "Natural Area," the state equivalent of a federal Wilderness Area.

Several variants of oak-hickory woodlands are dominant vegetation at the Shaw Nature Reserve. The property has typical Ozark woodlands that vary in composition according to drainage, moisture, pH, and aspect. Soil on wooded hilltops is drier, thinner, and occasionally rocky where it meets the glade. Typical of our region, about ten oaks and five hickories make up the majority of tree species and are complemented by a wonderful diversity of other trees, herbaceous plants, fungi, and animals. These woodlands, as reported by early naturalists, surveyors, and travelers in the 1800s, were originally much more open than those we are familiar with today.

A hike from the Trail House heads south toward the Meramec River and leads through upland forest, past Long Glade, and then winds down to reveal a dramatically different type of woodland.

Photo by Sonya Baerek

Photo by Kathryn LeRon

Photos by Scott Woodbury and Dany Brown

The Shaw Nature Reserve woodland is beautiful in all four seasons, whether dappled with pink redbud (Cercis canadensis) in spring or blazing with fall colors. The oak-hickory forest also hosts abundant wildlife. White-tailed deer, fox squirrels (Scurius niger), and wild turkey are commonly seen since they feed on acorns and hickory nuts. The red-headed woodpecker (Melanerpes erythrocephalus) also makes its home. Less commonly, nocturnal bobcat, raccoon, opossum, coyote, skunk—and even the stray armadillo!—have been sighted.

Seen here in the Whitmire Wildflower Garden beside a planting of ostrich fern (Matteucia struthipteris), *native persimmon trees* (Diospyros virginiana) *are a highly adaptable species that inhabits all of the woodland and forest variants at the Reserve. The fruits are relished by coyotes, who spread the seeds in their droppings as they roam over all parts of the landscape in quest of their varied diet.*

Watersheds extend down the slope and, at the lower elevations, run through moister soil where oaks and hickories give way to denser forest of sycamore, silver maple, cottonwood, and elm. Nutrients and moisture are plentiful in the alluvial soil, and frequent flooding is common in this bottomland forest. Here, too, a spectacular floral carpet appears each spring, delighting visitors who venture down the trail. Along the northern border one can see occasional bluffs, rock worn down by ancient rains and flowing water, indicating earlier courses of the river.

The woodlands are part of the active ecological restoration and habitat management program at the Reserve. Vigilant staff and volunteers have been seeking out and removing invasive species such as bush honeysuckle *(Lonicera maackii)*. Existing cedars are removed by logging to allow desirable herbaceous species the chance to thrive. In the woodlands, undesirable species are fire-sensitive, and their re-growth is inhibited with carefully controlled burns. These ongoing activities create a more diverse community, favoring the herbaceous woodland plants that blanket the forest floor.

In 2003, nearly 150 acres of the Shaw Nature Reserve bottomland woodland and gravel bars associated with the Meramec River shoreline were designated a "Natural Area," the state equivalent of a federal Wilderness Area. It was nominated due to its "rare and best regional representation of original Meramec River bottomland forest."

Photo by Scott Woodbury

Behind the Scenes

All that the Shaw Nature Reserve is today wouldn't have been possible without the consistent support of many donors, partners, and friends. For a list of these important people and organizations through the years, see page 92.

Partnerships

The potential for enhancing the environmental and educational programs at the Shaw Nature Reserve continues to be realized through partnerships with organizations having similar goals. Partnerships further the mission of both the Shaw Nature Reserve and the affiliated organization by making use of a broader base of facilities and staff. Through collaboration, the sum of these efforts creates stronger results.

For eight years and counting, the Shaw Nature Reserve has partnered with the Missouri Department of Conservation (MDC) and its Grow Native! program. The partnership launched in 2002, when MDC approached the Reserve about helping advance its focus on the use of native plants in the landscape. The complementary missions of the Reserve and MDC have resulted in a variety of successful collaborative projects over the years. Working with the Reserve's horticulture department, MDC provided funding for increased horticultural education to both the gardening and professional horticultural public. Thus was eventually born the Native Plant School, which continues to thrive and grow in popularity, with new topics added each year.

The annual Spring Wildflower Sale in May is just one of several initiatives to promote native plants to home gardeners and professional landscapers. In conjunction with the Missouri Department of Conservation, the Reserve offers Grow Native! programming, the Native Plant School, tours, and training.

Presented in partnership with the Missouri Department of Conservation, the biannual Prairie Day portrays prairie heritage, both pioneer and Native American, on the Reserve's 250-acre restored tall-grass prairie. Visitors play pioneer games, visit teepees, witness authentic craft demonstrations by weavers, spinners, basket-makers, and more.

MDC and the Reserve reinforced their commitment to conservation by working together to expand education and outreach programs at the Reserve. A biannual Prairie Day event, the Master Naturalist program, the Discover Nature–Women weekend, First Time Fishing for Kids, and the Native Plant Conference are but a few of the successful events. Indeed, much of the recent progress at the Reserve is a result of the continued support of MDC. The completion of the Edgar Anderson Center in 2010 allows office space for MDC education and outreach staff, and thus the continued growth of this rich collaboration.

Another major partner is the Tyson Research Center of Washington University in St. Louis. The Shaw Institute for Field Training (SIFT) is a result of this partnership and funding from the National Science Foundation. The program engages upper-level high-school students in the experiences of field biology and environmental studies, from seed collecting to stream quality monitoring. Students acquire valuable experience with the chance to gain hands-on practical experience in both field research and science communications as they present reports showcasing their work. This introduction to environmental and ecological fields of study offers the students an immersion in the natural world with the hope of inspiring many to focus their studies and work in environmental biology. SIFT also provides professional training for outreach educators.

First Time Fishing for Kids is another joint program of the Reserve and the Missouri Department of Conservation. The Reserve's ponds provide guaranteed success for these youngsters, who learn the fine points of fishing in a beautiful outdoor setting.

Maintenance

While the glamour often goes to those whose name is on the building, or those who interact directly with the public, the daily details of operations at the Reserve run smoothly thanks to the constant dedication of a talented crew of staff and volunteers. On any given day, the chatter on staff two-way radios includes all sorts of behind-the-scenes activity—where to mow, organize a controlled burn, a call to fix a vehicle, pipe, or electric line.

The Shaw Nature Reserve's Maintenance Department, with its team of seven full-time and one part-time staff and several volunteers, provides the necessary manpower for removing invasive species, restoring and managing habitat areas, constructing and maintaining bridges and boardwalks, benches, and picnic tables. Much of the construction of the Whitmire Wildflower Garden, wetland complex, and Dana Brown Overnight Center required their assistance. They don regulation burn suits and equipment for the prescribed burns that are an essential part of habitat management at the Reserve. Every building sparkles and never lacks a fresh coat of paint. Paths and trails are mowed and trimmed, and for the many special events held on the property, they put tents up, direct traffic and parking, then take down and store the tents until the next occasion. It is the behind-the-scenes dedication of the Maintenance team that creates the pleasant and safe environment visitors enjoy without realizing it.

First hired as summer help in 1981, Glenn Beffa (top) is now the General Operations Supervisor, overseeing the Reserve's Maintenance Department. This talented crew of staff and volunteers does everything from rocking the roads to clearing the snow to constructing and maintaining bridges, boardwalks, and benches. They also plan and conduct the prescribed burns of prairie and woodlands each winter.

Master Gardener volunteer Mary Ellen Mitchell gathers seed on the Shaw Nature Reserve prairie in late summer. In 2009, over 120 volunteers donated their time, talents, and perspiration to the Reserve.

Volunteers

Shaw Nature Reserve volunteers come from a diverse range of backgrounds and skills, yet it is what they have in common—a love of nature and a commitment to sharing it with others—that brings them together at the Reserve. The success of programs and projects conducted at the Reserve continues to be possible because of many talented volunteers who have generously contributed their time throughout the years. Volunteers devote their time, assisting with educational programs, wildflower walks, greenhouse and garden work, and collecting and sowing seed.

The Teacher Naturalists, a specific group of volunteers, receive ongoing training at the Shaw Nature Reserve. Once trained, these volunteers assist the education staff primarily with many children's outdoor educational programs, helping to instruct while offering young students the opportunity to experience and investigate the natural world. Other volunteers are Master Gardeners, donating hours in exchange for their Master Gardener training.

Wildflower walks in the 1970s and 1980s were led by avid wildflower and bird enthusiasts of the area—including Art Christ, Edgar Denison, Father Jim Sullivan, Nell Menke, and Betty Nellums—all of whom volunteered their time to share their passion for the natural world. They introduced many people to the joys and wonders of a simple walk at the Reserve observing native plants, birds, butterflies, and other wildlife. These walks were later expanded into a variety of education classes for both adults and children.

Among the most dedicated volunteers were some former employees. Retirement came, yet they felt compelled to stay on and continue the work they had begun. One such employee was Ray Garlick, employed at the Reserve in the 1970s and, for several years, the only maintenance employee. After retiring in 1984 at the age of seventy-two, Ray continued on as a volunteer for another twelve years. He could be seen most often on a tractor mowing in the warm months

Ray Garlick

and was always there to stoke the woodstove in the Maintenance Department on cold mornings. He and his wife resided in the Gate House at the main entrance to the Reserve, and during this time Ray was the official "gate keeper," opening and closing the visitors' gate on schedule every day. The Garlicks also donated the funds necessary to build a bridge at the north end of Pinetum Lake, a way of giving to visitors for many years to come.

Another notable volunteer was Rus Goddard, who was first introduced to

Rus Goddard

the Reserve at age eighteen by the first director, Lars Peter Jensen. Very much an outdoorsman, Rus volunteered well into his eighties, hiking and maintaining

the miles of trails at the Reserve. Searching for downed trees and branches, and armed with pruners and saws, he saw to it that the paths were kept clear for all to enjoy. Ray Garlick and Rus Goddard were both awarded the Garden's Career Service Award in 1997. This award is given to volunteers who have "repeatedly made substantial contributions over a number of years." Together these extraordinary men made a mark not only on the trails and fields at the Reserve but in the hearts of all those who worked with them.

Top
Full-time employee Helen McCallie staffs the Visitor Center and is the official greeter of most visitors to the Reserve. She joined the staff in 1996 and now oversees a dozen volunteers who help run the Visitor Center and book shop and who lead the Wilderness Wagon tours.

Bottom
A Boy Scout troop builds a bridge over a prairie swale in the Whitmire Wildflower Garden. School groups, scouting, and community service organizations have all found interesting volunteer opportunities at the Reserve.

FORGING AHEAD

The resemblance of this inchworm (moth family Geometridae) to a small green twig fails to provide camouflage on its brilliantly colored background of purple coneflower (Echinacea purpurea) *in the Whitmire Wildflower Garden.*

The current, unfolding chapter of the Shaw Nature Reserve that began with the 1990 master plan is perhaps the most exciting in its history. We, as a society, are only now beginning to realize just how much biodiversity has been lost, replaced by human landscapes. Suburban sprawl is fast encroaching on this once remote, rural property. This fact is the driving force behind most of the activities and programs at the Reserve. John Behrer, director of the Shaw Nature Reserve, states, "Our duty is to be good stewards of the 2,441 acres here, to restore and maintain the biological diversity, make it accessible, and to use it for education."

This focus is always present and at the core of expansion and progress at the Shaw Nature Reserve. The Reserve is a valuable resource for teaching people how to be good stewards of the natural world and foster an understanding of our place in it.

With eyes fixed on the future, the importance of places like the Shaw Nature Reserve becomes even more critical. Originally a day's trip from urban St. Louis, the Reserve is now just 30-40 minutes away, making it more accessible to this major metropolitan area. So much progress has been made to create and maintain the natural diversity that it serves as a premier sanctuary for

Edgar Anderson Center

Photo by Karen Hill

Named in honor of the former Missouri Botanical Garden director, the Edgar Anderson Center features energy-efficient offices and warehouse space for all of the Reserve's administrative operations.

Dedicated in 2010, the new Edgar Anderson Center at the Shaw Nature Reserve consists of three buildings (18,000 square feet) housing the Reserve's education, horticulture, and maintenance operations. In addition, the new facilities provide office space for Missouri Department of Conservation education and outreach staff, increasing opportunities for collaboration. Made possible in part through donations to the Missouri Botanical Garden's *Stewards of the Earth* capital campaign, the center was named in honor of former Garden director Edgar Anderson, a botanist and educator who had an abiding interest in introducing the public to the wonders of nature at the Reserve (see page 27).

The Reserve is pursuing LEED certification for this complex for its innovative sustainable construction as well as operation. The buildings boast passive solar features, energy-efficient lighting, and a novel cooling system that uses about half the energy of a conventional system. Rainfall from the roofs is collected in a cistern (originally constructed in 1927 for watering the orchids) to be used as part of the cooling system and for watering plants. A 50,000-square-foot storm-water retention wetland planted with native species captures runoff from the parking lot and other paved surfaces. The center replaced facilities that were built in the 1920s. During demolition of the old buildings, over 90 percent of the materials were either salvaged for reuse or recycled, reducing the amount of materials that had to be taken to landfills.

Illustration by Simon Oswald Architecture

Located just south of the Bascom House and Whitmire Wildflower Garden, the new Myron Glassberg Family Pavilions will serve schoolchildren, adult tour groups, and the general public.

not only indigenous plants and animals but for people as well. Management is ongoing and intensive in order to develop new areas and maintain existing ones in ways most representative of their natural origins. The objective is to develop the Shaw Nature Reserve to its fullest biological potential and at the same time to provide a habitat development model for others. Far from the hectic and highly technical modern world, children and adults will continue to have a natural place to enjoy.

The continued expansion of programs and projects and the associated staff increase at the Shaw Nature Reserve was foreseen in the 1990 master plan. Included in the plan was a new building, at first called the Environmental Support Complex, which would serve as an efficient home base for the education, horticulture, and maintenance departments. This complex, dedicated as the Edgar Anderson Center, was completed in 2010.

Another component of the master plan is a new visitor center. A site has been selected near the Bascom House looking out over prairie to woodlands beyond and designed to blend with the surrounding landscape.

We work in a beautiful place that we never take for granted. To share it with visitors is a privilege.

–Lydia Toth, Senior Manager of Education

Utilizing energy-efficient systems such as solar power and water recycling as well as a low-maintenance landscape, the new visitor center will illustrate various ways to create efficient and sustainable structures. It is hoped that construction will begin during the next decade.

In an effort to amplify the effects of the work being done at the Reserve, staff are attentive to increasing the possibilities of partnerships with like-minded organizations. In this way, resources can be shared in order to expand environmental programs and opportunities in the community and region. From conservation and education to recreation, the Shaw Nature Reserve has only just begun to fulfill its potential as an environmental resource.

Establishing relationships with communities in order to assist in planning and development will take habitat restoration and native plant landscaping to the next level. The use of native plants in our landscapes provides solutions to many of the challenges that face modern development, from storm-water runoff mitigation to minimizing irrigation and mowing. Continued expansion of the Native Plant School and associated events will further horticultural education of homeowners and professionals alike. In this way, the Shaw Nature Reserve can help create a proactive approach to development, working with communities at all levels.

Since the second half of the twentieth century, people have been increasingly conscious of the need to preserve species of plants, animals, fungi, and microorganisms—biodiversity—to sustain the land on which they grow and the biological communities that they comprise. The dedication of the staff and volunteers at the Shaw Nature Reserve is best illustrated by Senior Manager of Education Lydia Toth's statement, "We work in a beautiful place that we never take for granted. To share it with visitors is a privilege." More and more visitors come to the Reserve every year to learn about the natural world and their place in it by exploring; hiking; and studying through taking classes, field trips, and research. Our need to connect with the natural world cannot be satisfied by images and movies alone, regardless of how well they are produced. Books cannot teach the experience and lessons of being in a wild space. The natural world reveals itself in many ways and at many different levels. And without a connection to the natural world, humankind grows emotionally stunted and more likely to destroy our precious resources. For the health of humanity and the health of the planet, it is imperative that places like the Shaw Nature Reserve be preserved for future generations. With eighty-five years of history and the support of the Missouri Botanical Garden, the community, our donors, partners, staff, and volunteers, the Shaw Nature Reserve should be around for a long time to come!

The Meramec River frontage on the Shaw Nature Reserve at sunrise. Part of the state-designated "Natural Area," it is considered one of the "best regional representations of original bottomland forest" in Missouri—and one of the most beautiful.

By The Numbers

The Shaw Nature Reserve has:

Photo by Scott Woodbury

a main entrance on historic Route 66

Photo by Sonya Buerck

a 5-acre wildflower garden, the largest in the region

14 miles of maintained hiking trails

2,441 acres

5 distinct habitats: glade, prairie, wetland, woodland, and forest

a 1.5-acre outdoor Nature Explore™ Classroom

nearly 1,200 species of plants

84 recorded species of butterflies

250 acres of restored tall-grass prairie

shawnature.org

Photo by Kevin Wolf

**a 32-acre wetland with
a 300-foot boardwalk**

Photo by Danny Brown

19 species of
oaks (10 native;
9 introduced)

deer, fox, coyote, bobcat,
rabbits, squirrels, skunks,
raccoons, opossum,
mink, weasels, beaver

**284 species of birds
(74% of the total in Missouri)**

1.5 miles of
frontage on
both sides of
the Meramec
River

147 acres of
bottomland forest
designated a State
Natural Area

72 recorded
species of
native ants

Map

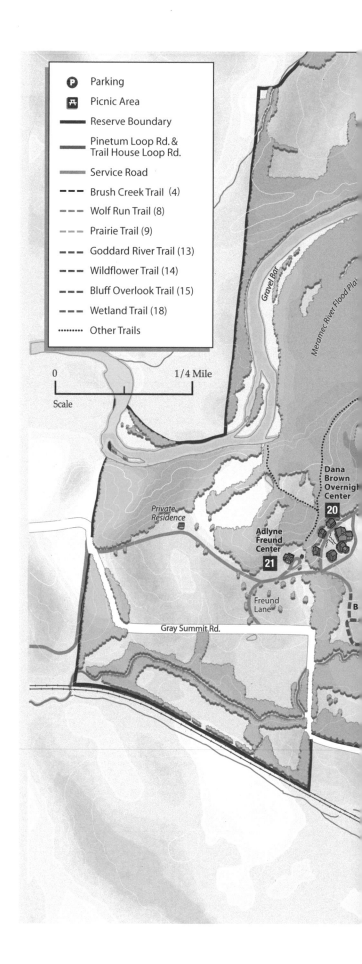

Meramec River

Gravel Bar

State
Natural Area **16**

Bluff Overlook   *Glade*

Prairie

14

12   *Glade*   *Private Property*

15   **Maritz Trail House**   **13**

11   Pine Amphitheater Rd.

Glade   *Prairie*   **Pine Amphitheater**

Prairie

Quarry Road

Mirror Lake   **10**   **Sod House**   Lumbershed Rd.

Observation Deck

Barn Road   **9**

Prairie

Glade

Pot Hole Lake

Freund Ridge Rd.

17   **Bus Stop**   Quail Demonstration Area

Prairie   **18**   **Cemetery**   Trail House Loop Rd.   **7**   Quail Trail

Observation Blind   *Prairie*   **6**   **Bascom House**

walk   *Wetland*   **5**   **Whitmire Wildflower Garden**

Brush Creek   **19**   **Serpentine Wall**   *Prairie*   **4**

Serpentine Wall Rd.   **8**   **3**

Edward K. Love Nursery   Nursery Road   *Pinetum Lake*   **22**

Private Residence   *Wolf Run Lake*   **2**   **Nature Explore Classroom**

Gray Summit Rd.   **Visitor Center**   HWY 100

Railroad   **1**

Main Entrance

Route 66/Osage Rd.   Hwy 100   **44**

Robertsville Road

People

Missouri Botanical Garden Presidents

Henry Shaw, 1859-1889
William Trelease, 1889-1912
George T. Moore, 1912-1953
Edgar S. Anderson, 1954-1956
Frits Went, 1958-1963
David Gates, 1965-1971
Peter H. Raven, 1971-2010
Peter Wyse Jackson, 2010-present

Shaw Nature Reserve Directors

Lars Peter Jensen, manager 1926-1941
August P. Bielmann, manager 1941-1956
Frank Steinberg, superintendent 1957-1970
David Goudy, superintendent 1971-1979
George U. Wise, superintendent, 1979-1983
John Behrer, director 1983-present

Shaw Nature Reserve Advisory Committee

L. B. Eckelkamp, Jr., *chair*
Daniel A. Burkhardt
Jennifer Dierking
Arnold W. Donald, *ex officio*
Mary Jane Fredrickson
Dr. Patricia Hagen
Robert E. Hansen
Paula M. Keinath
Charles E. Kopman
Doug Ladd
Dr. Pamela McIntyre
Parker B. McMillan
John C. McPheeters
William L. Miller, Sr.
James D. Minton
David T. Orthwein
Glee Stanley
Sheila Steelman
Blanton J. Whitmire, *emeritus*

Shaw Nature Reserve Staff*

John Behrer, *director*
Aileen Abbott
Catrina Adams
Glenn Beffa
Terri Brandt
Karen Bryan
Robert Bryan
Gregory Caldwell
Diane Donovan
Vivian Freer
Judith Hunt
Jennifer Lee
Helen McCallie
David Middleton
Jerry Pemberton
Besa Schweitzer
Erin Sleeper
Jeffrey Smith
Robert Stokes
Dennis Thurman
Lydia Toth
James Trager
Barbara Troutman
Scott Woodbury
Katie Zimmer

*As of June 1, 2010.

Overleaf
A panorama of Pinetum Lake. (Photo by Scott Avetta.)

Thank you!

The Missouri Botanical Garden gratefully acknowledges the following donors for their generous major gifts in support of the Shaw Nature Reserve over the years.*

AmeriCorps National Civilian Conservation Corps
Bascom Charitable Trust
Estate of Elizabeth Evans Bascom
Estate of Mary Elizabeth Bascom
Mr. and Mrs. Joseph H. Bascom
Mr. Louis G. Brenner, Jr.
Mr. and Mrs. Robert Bronstein
Dana Brown Charitable Trust
The Casa Audlon Lead Annuity Trust
Mrs. Marilyn K. Chryst
Commerce Bancshares, Inc.
Mr. and Mrs. Henry P. Day
Mr. and Mrs. L. B. Eckelkamp, Jr.
Federated Garden Clubs of Missouri, Inc.
Gateway Foundation
Clifford Willard Gaylord Foundation
Mrs. Myron Glassberg
Allen P. and Josephine B. Green Foundation
Ms. Elizabeth L. Green
Jane Freund Harris
Whitney and Anna Harris
Dr. and Mrs. August Homeyer
Estate of August Homeyer
Mr. and Mrs. Jack A. Jacobs
The William T. Kemper Foundation –
      Commerce Bank, Trustee
Mr. and Mrs. Charles R. Klauke

Mr. and Mrs. S. Lee Kling
Estate of F. B. and B. A. Krukoff
June M. and Fred S. Kummer, Jr.
Mr. and Mrs. E. Desmond Lee, Jr.
Mr. and Mrs. John S. Lehmann
David B. Lichtenstein Foundation
Ms. Leslie Limberg and Mr. Leo M. Steck
John Allan Love Charitable Foundation
Edward K. Love Conservation Foundation
Mr. and Mrs. Carlyle A. Luer
Estate of William E. Maritz
Maritz Inc.
Mr. and Mrs. John C. McPheeters
Missouri Department of Conservation
Missouri Department of Natural Resources
Mr. and Mrs. Lucius B. Morse III
National Fish and Wildlife Foundation
National Park Service
Mrs. Raoul R. Pantaleoni
Mr. and Mrs. A. Timon Primm III
Mrs. Jean H. Sachs
Ms. Carolyn Susann Schwaab
Family of Frank Steinberg
Norman J. Stupp Foundation –
      Commerce Bank, Trustee
The Trio Foundation of St. Louis
Robert J. Trulaske, Jr. Family Foundation
U.S. Army Corps of Engineers
Mr. and Mrs. Mahlon B. Wallace III
Mr. and Mrs. Blanton J. Whitmire

* Some donors wish to remain anonymous.

Commemorate your family milestones with a gift to the Shaw Nature Reserve. Contact the Office of Institutional Advancement for more details at (314) 577-9500 or visit www.mobot.org and click on "Ways to Give."

INDEX